Revise

Author: Heather Murphy

Audio for Speaking and Listening at your fingertips

Scan the audio QR codes to immediately launch high-quality recordings of native speakers. These are exam-style tracks for realistic assessment practice and can particularly help you with:

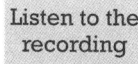

- **Listening: Dictation task practice**
  Listen in full, then in parts, then in full, for exam-style practice.
- **Speaking: Reading aloud practice**
  Targeted pronunciation practice of sounds helps build your confidence.
- **Speaking: Role play practice**
  Hear the teacher part and speak your answers in the pauses.

Transcripts for all audio files can be accessed here.

Support for longer writing tasks

Space is provided in this Workbook but sometimes you'll need to use your own paper too. Full sample student responses are given in the answer section so that you can self-assess. Remember that there is more than one correct answer for this type of question.

Practice papers

Help to check that you are exam-ready with a full set of practice papers containing exam-style questions for Listening, Speaking, Reading and Writing, for both Foundation and Higher tier.

Higher and Foundation tiers

Content that only applies to Higher Tier is marked with an **H** (only).

Difficulty scale

The icon next to each exam-style question tells you how difficult it is.

Some questions cover a range of difficulties.

Target grade 4

Target grade 7-8

Also available:

The Revision Guide helps you revise vocabulary and grammar with a manageable topic-by-topic approach. Worked example questions and pages on each exam paper will build your skills ready for assessment, and digital resources such as quick quizzes, vocab checks, videos and flashcards are all included!

AQA publishes the only official Sample Assessment Material on its website. The questions in this Workbook have been designed to familiarise you with the type of tasks you may meet in the exam, and are tailored to help you to practise specific skills. Remember that the actual assessments may not look like this.

Contents

Identity and relationships with others
1. Physical descriptions
2. Character descriptions
3. My family
4. Friends
5. Relationships
6. Dealing with problems
7. Daily routine
8. Clothing and fashion
9. Identity
10. When I was younger
11. My life in the future

Healthy living and lifestyle
12. Food and drink
13. Meals at home
14. Shopping for food
15. Eating out
16. A healthy diet
17. Sporting events
18. Advantages of sport
19. Physical wellbeing
20. Mental wellbeing
21. Feeling unwell
22. Avoiding health risks

Education and work
23. My school
24. School subjects
25. My teachers
26. The school day
27. School uniform
28. School rules
29. Homework
30. Stress at school
31. My ideal school
32. Preparing for exams
33. Gap year
34. Plans for next year
35. Future studies
36. Future career
37. Opinions about jobs

Free-time activities
38. Free-time activities
39. Music and dance
40. Arranging to go out
41. Reading
42. Television
43. Film and cinema

Customs, festivals and celebrations
44. Celebrations
45. Customs and festivals
46. Places of interest
47. Traditions
48. Learning languages

Celebrity culture
49. Celebrity culture
50. Opinions about being a celebrity
51. Sports stars
52. Celebrity events
53. Celebrities for the environment

Travel and tourism
54. Holiday activities
55. Holiday accommodation
56. Other holiday accommodation
57. Opinions about travelling
58. Planning a future holiday
59. Past holidays
60. Holiday problems
61. Making a complaint
62. Lost property
63. Holiday jobs
64. Buying gifts and souvenirs

Media and technology
65. Mobile technology
66. Social media
67. Internet
68. Computer games
69. Opinions about technology
70. Films on the internet

The environment and where people live
71. My home
72. My town
73. Facilities in town
74. Finding the way
75. Shops and shopping
76. Shopping in town
77. Transport
78. Travelling by train
79. The environment and me
80. Environmental problems
81. The dangers of pollution
82. Individual actions for the environment
83. How to recycle
84. Weather
85. The natural world

About the exams
86. Practice for Paper 1: Listening
87. Practice for Paper 1: Listening
88. Practice for Paper 2: Speaking
89. Practice for Paper 2: Speaking
90. Practice for Paper 3: Reading
91. Practice for Paper 3: Reading
92. Practice for Paper 4: Writing
93. Practice for Paper 4: Writing

Grammar
94. Gender and plurals
95. Indefinite articles and possessives
96. Nominative and accusative cases
97. Other cases and prepositions
98. Prepositions with the accusative or dative
99. *Dieser*, *jeder* and *welcher*
100. Adjective endings
101. Comparative and superlative adjectives and adverbs
102. Personal pronouns
103. Word order 1
104. Conjunctions
105. Word order 2
106. The present tense
107. Reflexive and separable verbs
108. Irregular verb tables 1
109. Irregular verb tables 2
110. Using irregular verbs in different tenses
111. *Sein* and *haben*
112. Modal verbs in the present tense
113. The perfect tense with *haben*
114. The perfect tense with *sein*
115. The imperfect tense
116. The future tense
117. The conditional

Practice papers
118. Paper 1: Listening (Foundation)
121. Paper 2: Speaking (Foundation)
122. Paper 3: Reading (Foundation)
127. Paper 4: Writing (Foundation)
128. Paper 1: Listening (Higher)
132. Paper 2: Speaking (Higher)
133. Paper 3: Reading (Higher)
139. Paper 4: Writing (Higher)

140. Answers

A small bit of small print

AQA publishes Sample Assessment Material and the Specification on its website. This is the official content and this book should be used in conjunction with it. The questions in this Workbook have been written to help you practise every topic in the book. Remember: the real exam questions may not look like this.

1-to-1 page match with the German Revision Guide ISBN 9781292739694

Had a go ☐ Nearly there ☐ Nailed it! ☐

Identity and relationships with others

Physical descriptions

Friends and family

1 Alina, Felix and Sascha are describing a friend or family member. What do they say?

Choose the correct answer and write the letter in each box.

> In the Listening exam, use the five minutes' preparation time to make a quick note of a few of the key words you might expect to hear. For Question 1(c) here, you might note *kleiner / schlanker / größer*, so you know what to listen out for.

Listen to the recording

(a) Alina's dad is …

A	tall and slim.
B	tall and slightly fat.
C	tall and sporty.

☐ (1 mark)

(b) He has …

A	short black hair.
B	short grey hair.
C	short dark brown hair.

☐ (1 mark)

(c) Felix's friend is …

A	smaller than Felix.
B	thinner than Felix.
C	taller than Felix.

☐ (1 mark)

(d) He has …

A	dark blue eyes.
B	brown eyes.
C	light blue eyes.

☐ (1 mark)

(e) Sascha's sister has …

A	long blonde hair.
B	small ears.
C	green eyes.

☐ (1 mark)

Translation

2 Translate the following sentences into **German**.

I am sixteen years old and quite tall.

....

I have short brown hair.

....

My friend has a round face and blue eyes.

....

My brothers are smaller than me.

....

She is pretty and looks sporty.

....

(10 marks)

> For the third sentence, you'll need an *er / sie / es* form to match *mein Freund* (he) / *meine Freundin* (she).

> Watch out: the fourth sentence has a plural subject!

1

Identity and relationships with others

Had a go ☐ Nearly there ☐ Nailed it! ☐

Character descriptions

Your family and friends

1 A German exchange student is coming to stay.

Write a short description of your family and friends for them.

Write approximately **50** words in **German**.

You must write something about each bullet point.

Mention:
- a positive characteristic you have
- a negative characteristic you have
- what a member of your family is like
- what your best friend is like
- what you do with friends.

> Aim to write about 10 words for each bullet point.

> If you have more to say about one bullet point than others, that's fine as the responses do not need to be of equal length.

> Check your work to make sure you have covered all the bullet points.

....
....
....
....
....
....
....

(10 marks)

Reading aloud

2 Read aloud the following text in **German**.

> Ich denke, dass ich meistens sehr freundlich bin.
> Ich versuche, zu anderen Leuten immer nett zu sein.
> In der Schule muss ich hart arbeiten, weil ich einige Fächer schwierig finde.
> Zu Hause bin ich ruhig und kann meine Freizeit genießen.
> Meine Eltern finden mich ehrlich und vertrauen mir total.

> You can listen to the audio in the Answers section to check your pronunciation.

(5 marks)

> Sounds to take note of here:
> - *a* – can be long or short; in *dass* it's short, but in *total* it's long
> - *v* – sounds like a soft 'f'
> - *z* – has a crisp 'ts' sound
> - *ei* – sounds like the English 'I'
> - *ä* – sounds like 'a' and 'e' combined
> - *schw* – sounds like 'shv'
> - *-e* – final 'e' is a sounded syllable.
> Listen to the recording to practise these sounds.

Track 2

Listen to the recording

Now play the recording of four questions in **German** related to the topic of **Identity and relationships with others**. In order to score the highest marks, you must try to answer all four questions as fully as you can.

(10 marks)

Had a go ☐ Nearly there ☐ Nailed it! ☐

Identity and relationships with others

My family

Describing my family

1 You read this post by a German teenager, Jana, on the subject of family.

> Ich habe eine ziemlich kleine Familie. Meine Eltern sind getrennt, und wir sind jetzt nur drei zu Hause. Es gibt meinen Bruder, Ben, meine Mutter, Linda, und mich. Wir haben auch eine kleine Katze. Wir sind meistens glücklich. Ben und ich haben viel gemeinsam, denn wir sind beide sehr aktiv und sportlich. Wir sind oft zusammen. Unsere Mutter hat lange Arbeitsstunden in einem Geschäft und hat nicht genug Zeit für uns, aber sie liebt uns sehr.

Complete these sentences. Write the letter for the correct option in each box.

(a) Jana's family is …

A	big.
B	small.
C	very big.

(1 mark)

(b) Jana has …

A	no pets.
B	a cat.
C	a dog.

(1 mark)

(c) Jana and her brother …

A	don't like sport.
B	have similar interests.
C	don't spend much time together.

(1 mark)

(d) Jana's mum …

A	is unemployed.
B	works from home.
C	works long hours.

(1 mark)

Photo card

2 Talk about the content of these photos. You must say at least **one** thing about each photo.

Photo 1

Photo 2

> Start by saying which people you can see in the photos. How old are they? What relation might they be to each other? What do they look like? What are they wearing? Then say where they are. If the photo is taken outside, you can comment on the weather too.

(5 marks)

Listen to the recording

> In the exam, the photo will be in black and white. However, you can still talk about colours. Here, you could say *Ein Mann trägt ein weißes Hemd.*

After you have spoken about the content of the photos, listen to the recording of further questions on the same topic. Pause the recording to give your answers.

(6 marks)

Identity and relationships with others

Had a go ☐ Nearly there ☐ Nailed it! ☐

Friends

Target grades 4–6

Your friends

1. You are writing about your friends.

   Write approximately **90** words in **German**.

   You must write something about each bullet point.

   Describe:
   - something about a good friend or friends
   - what you have done recently with friends
   - what you plan to do with friends next weekend.

   > Note that this question has three bullet points, the first in the present tense, the second in the past tense and the third in the future tense.

   > Opinions are always better if you can explain them using *denn* or *weil*!

   ....
   ....
   ....
   ....
   ....
   ....
   ....
   ....
   ....
   ....
   ....
   ....
   ....

   (15 marks)

Target grades 5–9

Role play

2. You are talking to your German friend.

   Listen to the recording of the teacher's part. The teacher will play the part of your friend and will speak first.

   You should address your friend as *du*.

   When you see this – ? – you will have to ask a question.

Listen to the recording

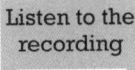

   > 1 Say something about your friends. (Give **two** details.)
   > ?2 Ask your German friend a question about their best friend.
   > 3 Say why good friends are important to you. (Give **two** details.)
   > 4 Say what you have done recently with your friends. (Give **two** details.)
   > 5 Say what your plans are for the weekend.

   (10 marks)

   > Remember: there are two marks for each task – extended answers are not required. You simply need to communicate the essential information in a sentence including an appropriate verb.

Had a go ☐ Nearly there ☐ Nailed it! ☐   **Identity and relationships with others**

Relationships

Family relationships

1 You read Robin's blog on a youth problem forum.

> Mit meiner Familie verstehe ich mich im Moment gar nicht gut, und ich finde es sehr schwierig, mit meinen Eltern zu reden. Sie wollen nicht zuhören, wenn ich versuche, mit ihnen ehrlich zu sein.
>
> Das Problem? Ich bin ihr einziger Sohn und ich bin gay. Ich habe auch einen netten Freund, den ich liebe, und das können sie nicht akzeptieren. Natürlich möchte ich eine bessere Beziehung zu meinen Eltern haben, aber das scheint unmöglich zu sein.

Answer the following questions in **English**.

(a) Describe Robin's current relationship with his parents. Give **two** details.

.... **(2 marks)**

(b) What happens when he tries to be honest with them?

.... **(1 mark)**

(c) What does Robin say is the problem? Give **two** details.

.... **(2 marks)**

(d) What can't his parents accept? Give **two** details.

.... **(2 marks)**

(e) What would Robin like to have?

.... **(1 mark)**

> Look at any indications about how much information you should give. An additional instruction guides you when you need to give more than one detail.

Translation

2 Translate the following sentences into **English**.

Ich habe viele nette Freunde.

.... **(2 marks)**

Ein guter Freund von mir ist sehr positiv und lustig.

.... **(2 marks)**

Ich mag ihn, weil er immer Zeit für mich hat.

.... **(2 marks)**

Wir machen jeden Tag unsere Hausaufgaben zusammen.

.... **(2 marks)**

Gestern haben wir Computerspiele gespielt.

.... **(2 marks)**

> Time markers can give you further clues to the tense, so pay attention to them – in the final sentence *Gestern* (yesterday) clearly has to be followed by a past tense verb.

Identity and relationships with others

Had a go ☐   Nearly there ☐   Nailed it! ☐

Dealing with problems

Target grades 1–2

Picture task

> You can often use *Es gibt* (there is / are) or *Ich sehe* (I can see) and use a verb in each sentence.

> You can describe the appearance of the people, their clothes, where they are and what they are doing.

1 You see this photo on social media.

　What is in this photo?

　Write **five** sentences in **German**.

　...
　...
　...
　...
　...

(10 marks)

Target grades 5–9

Photo card

2 Talk about the content of these photos. You must say at least **one** thing about each photo.

(5 marks)

Photo 1

Photo 2

> Good starting points for describing the photos are:
> - How many people, male or female, young or old.
> - What they are wearing, if they are happy or sad.
> - Where they are, indoors or outdoors, in town, etc.
> - What they are doing, eating, laughing. Are they swimming, arguing …?
> - In the exam, the photos will be in black and white. However, you can still talk about colours.

Listen to the recording

After you have spoken about the content of the photos, listen to the recording of further questions on the same topic. Pause the recording to give your answers.

(20 marks)

> Remember that in the exam, there will be an extended unprepared conversation around the theme. These three example questions simply give you an idea of what to expect.

Had a go ☐ **Nearly there** ☐ **Nailed it!** ☐

Identity and relationships with others

Daily routine

A typical day

1 You are writing to a Swiss friend about a typical day.

Write approximately **90** words in **German**.
You must write something about each bullet point.

Describe:
- your weekday morning routine
- how you got to school yesterday
- what you will do this weekend.

> Remember to respond to each bullet point in the appropriate tense. For this question, the first bullet point will be in the present, the second in the past and the third in the future tense.

....
....
....
....
....
....
....
....
....
.... **(15 marks)**

Reading aloud

2 Read aloud the following text in **German**.

> Ich stehe immer spät auf.
> Ich ziehe mich schnell an.
> Zum Frühstück esse ich oft Brot und Obst.
> Um Viertel vor sieben muss ich das Haus verlassen.
> Dann fahre ich mit dem Fahrrad zur Schule.

(5 marks)

> Listen to these sounds to help you get the pronunciation right:
> - *st* – say 'sht'
> - *ä* – imagine an 'a' with an 'e' sound after it
> - *ü* – combines 'u' and 'e', try pursing your lips and say 'u'
> - *z* – say 'ts'
> - *v* – say a soft 'f'
> - final *-d* in *Fahrrad* – say it like a 't'
> - final *-e* in *Schule* – pronounce the 'e' as a separate syllable.

Track 7

Listen to the recording

Now play the recording to listen to and answer four questions in **German** that relate to the topic of **Identity and relationships with others**.

In order to score the highest marks, you must try to **answer all four questions as fully as you can**.

(10 marks)

7

Identity and relationships with others

Had a go ☐ Nearly there ☐ Nailed it! ☐

Clothing and fashion

Picture task

1 You see this photo on Instagram.

   What is in this photo?

   Write **five** sentences in **German**.

   ....
   ....
   ....
   ....
   ....

   (10 marks)

Dictation

2 Play the recording of five short sentences.

   Listen carefully and using your knowledge of German sounds, write down in **German** exactly what you hear for each sentence.

   You will hear each sentence **three** times: the first time as a full sentence, the second time in short sections and the third time again as a full sentence.

   Use your knowledge of German sounds and grammar to make sure that what you have written makes sense. Check carefully that your spelling is accurate.

   Sentence 1
   ....

   Sentence 2
   ....

   Sentence 3
   ....

   Sentence 4
   ....

   Sentence 5
   ....

   (10 marks)

> Remember that the dictation text will include two words which are not on the vocabulary list and with which you may not be familiar.

> Here are some key sounds to listen out for:
> - *sch* – sounds like 'sh'
> - *ü* – sounds like 'u' and 'e' combined
> - *u* – sounds like 'oo'
> - final *-e* – this is a sounded syllable (*diese*)
> - *qu* – sounds like 'kv' (*bequem*)
> - final *-ig* – sounds more like *ich* (*wichtig*)
> - *v* – sounds like 'f' (*Vater*)
> - *ä* – sounds like an 'a' combined with an 'e' (*trägt*).
>
> Listen to the recording to practise these sounds.

Track 10

Had a go ☐   **Nearly there** ☐   **Nailed it!** ☐

Identity and relationships with others

Identity

Grammar task

1 Using your knowledge of grammar, complete the following sentences in **German**. Choose the correct German word from the three options in the grid. Write the correct **word** in the space, as shown in the example below.

    Example:

    Ich .....gehe...... gern in die Stadt.

geht	gehe	gehen

This is an example of Foundation Question 3. It is a short test of your knowledge of basic German grammar. You will need to apply what you know about subject and verb forms, adjective endings, genders and cases.

(a) Mein bester Freund .... sehr nett.

sind	ist	bist

(1 mark)

(b) .... hilft mir mit meinen Mathehausaufgaben.

Er	Ich	Du

(1 mark)

(c) Wir .... oft zusammen Tennis.

spielst	spielen	spielt

(1 mark)

(d) Ich habe eine .... Familie.

großen	großes	große

(1 mark)

(e) Ich interessiere .... für Kleidung.

mich	dich	sich

(1 mark)

About myself

2 You are writing to an Austrian friend about yourself.
   Write approximately **90** words in **German**.
   You must write something about each bullet point.

   Describe:

   • what is important to you in life
   • an occasion when you have helped a friend
   • what your plans are for this weekend.

   ....
   ....
   ....
   ....
   ....
   ....
   ....

(15 marks)

Identity and relationships with others

Had a go ☐ Nearly there ☐ Nailed it! ☐

When I was younger

Reading aloud

1 Read aloud the following text in **German**.

> Als Kind habe ich in einem Dorf gewohnt.
> Ich habe jeden Tag Fußball gespielt.
> Ich ging gern mit meinen Eltern schwimmen.
> Meine Schule war sehr klein.
> Die Lehrer waren immer nett und freundlich.

Sounds to take note of here:
- -d – sounds like 't'
- j – sounds like 'y'
- ie – sounds like the English 'ee'
- schw – sounds like 'shv'
- ei – sounds like the English 'I'.
- w – sounds like 'v'

Listen to the recording to practise these sounds.

Track 11

Listen to the recording

Now play the recording to listen to and answer four questions in **German** that relate to the topic of **Identity and relationships with others**.

In order to score the highest marks, you must try to **answer all four questions as fully as you can**.

(10 marks)

Photo card

2 Talk about the content of these photos. You must say at least **one** thing about each photo.

(5 marks)

Photo 1

Photo 2

Listen to the recording

After you have spoken about the content of the photos, listen to the recording of further questions on the topic of **People and lifestyle**. Pause the recording to give your answers. There is a sample recording in the Answers section to give you more ideas.

(20 marks)

> Remember that in the exam, there will be an extended unprepared conversation around the theme. These three example questions simply give you an idea of what to expect.

Had a go ☐   Nearly there ☐   Nailed it! ☐

Identity and relationships with others

My life in the future

Target grades 1–5

Dictation

Listen to the recording

1 Play the recording of four short sentences.

Listen carefully and using your knowledge of German sounds, write down in **German** exactly what you hear for each sentence.

You will hear each sentence **three** times: the first time as a full sentence, the second time in short sections and the third time again as a full sentence.

Use your knowledge of German sounds and grammar to make sure that what you have written makes sense. Check carefully that your spelling is accurate.

Sentence 1 ....

Sentence 2 ....

Sentence 3 ....

Sentence 4 ....   **(8 marks)**

> Here are some key sounds to listen out for:
> - ä – sounds like a combination of 'a' and 'e'
> - st – sounds like 'sht'
> - w – sounds like 'v'
> - j – sounds like 'y'
> - ö – sounds like a combination of 'o' and 'e'.
> Listen to the recording to practise these sounds.

Track 15

Target grades 5–9

My life now and future plans

2 You are writing a post on a German online forum.

Your post is about your life now and your future plans.

Write approximately **150** words in **German**.

You must write something about both bullet points.

Describe:
- what your life is like now
- what your plans are for the future.

> Here, the first bullet point is in the present tense; the second will always be in either the future or the past time frame.

....

....

....

....

....

....

....

....

> Continue your answer on your own paper if you do not have space here.

(25 marks)

Healthy living and lifestyle

Had a go ☐ Nearly there ☐ Nailed it! ☐

Food and drink

Planning a meal

1 You hear Noah and his boyfriend Tim planning a meal for Sunday.

Complete the sentences in **English**.

Write **one** word in each space.

Example: Noah checks that Tim has bought ......*meat*...... .

(a) They still need to buy .... this afternoon. **(1 mark)**

(b) Noah asks whether they need anything else for the .... **(1 mark)**

(c) Tim suggests they should buy .... **(1 mark)**

> It is clear from the context and the gapped sentences that this conversation is about food. On the first listen, try to jot down each food item you hear in the right order, to help you work out the answers.

Eating habits

2 You hear Ben talking about food.

What does he say?

Choose the correct answer and write the letter in each box.

(a) What is Ben's attitude to food?

A	He is a food fanatic.
B	He is a keen cook.
C	He is not very interested in food.

☐ **(1 mark)**

(b) What does Ben enjoy eating?

A	He likes sausages.
B	He likes fruit.
C	He likes cake.

☐ **(1 mark)**

(c) What did they eat yesterday?

A	They ate chicken and salad.
B	They ate fish and chips.
C	They ate chicken and chips.

☐ **(1 mark)**

> The questions give you some ideas about the food-related words you will hear. Before the recording starts, it's a good idea to take a moment to think what these words would be in German, to help you identify them once the recording starts.

Had a go ☐   Nearly there ☐   Nailed it! ☐

Healthy living and lifestyle

Meals at home

Translation

1 Translate these sentences into **English**.

Ich esse nicht gern Gemüse.

....

Morgens trinke ich schwarzen Kaffee, der lecker ist.

....

Mein Vater kocht jeden Tag das Abendessen.

....

Gestern haben wir Wurst mit Brot gegessen.

....

Wenn ich Hunger habe, esse ich gern Pommes.

.... **(10 marks)**

Reading aloud

2 Read aloud the following text in **German**.

> Ich bin Vegetarierin und esse deshalb kein Fleisch und keinen Fisch.
> Ich esse jeden Morgen ein gutes Frühstück, denn das gibt mir Energie.
> Meiner Meinung nach ist es das wichtigste Essen des Tages.
> Ich gehe nie aus dem Haus, bevor ich gegessen habe.
> Mein Lieblingsessen ist ein Obstkuchen, den meine Mutti macht.

(5 marks)

> You may wish to use some of the preparation time to write out the whole reading aloud text and annotate it with any key pronunciation issues. If you choose to do this, you could also mark any pauses where you can take a breath – and aim to read at a steady pace, rather than rushing though the reading.

Listen to the recording

Now play the recording to listen to and answer four questions in **German** related to the topic of **Healthy living and lifestyle**.

In order to score the highest marks, you must try to **answer all four questions as fully as you can**.

(10 marks)

> Sounds to take note of here:
> - *g* – a hard sound, so not like the English 'j'
> - *ei* – sounds like the English 'I'
> - *j* – sounds like 'y'
> - short *e* – as in *denn*
> - *v* – a soft 'f' sound.
> Listen to the recording to practise these sounds.

Track 19

13

Healthy living and lifestyle

Had a go ☐   Nearly there ☐   Nailed it! ☐

Shopping for food

Role play

1 You are talking to your Swiss friend.

Listen to the recording of the teacher's part. The teacher will play the part of your friend and will speak first.

You should address your friend as *du*.

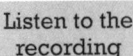

When you see this – ? – you will have to ask a question.

> In order to score full marks, you must include a verb in your response to each task.

> 1 Say what you like to eat.
> 2 Say what you think about vegetarian food.
> 3 Say what the food is like at school.
> 4 Say what you eat in the evenings.
> ?5 Ask your friend a question about buying food.

(10 marks)

> For one task at Foundation tier you will need to ask a simple question – practise how to do this!

Translation

2 Translate the following sentences into **German**.

I often help my grandmother with shopping.

....

It is not easy for her to carry heavy bags.

....

On Saturday morning, we went to the big supermarket in town.

....

After lunch at a café, we bought fruit and vegetables at the market.

....

If I have time, I will also cook the evening meal.

....

(10 marks)

Had a go ☐ Nearly there ☐ Nailed it! ☐

Healthy living and lifestyle

Eating out

In a restaurant

1 You hear this conversation in a restaurant.

What does each person want to eat?

Write the correct letter in each box.

A	cake
B	cheese
C	chicken
D	fish
E	sausage
F	vegetables

(a) Tim ☐

(b) Hanna ☐

(c) Mohamed ☐

(d) Alina ☐

(4 marks)

Reviewing a meal

2 Two people are discussing their restaurant meal.

What opinions do they have about the experience?

Write **P** for a **positive** opinion

    N for a **negative** opinion

    P+N for a **positive** and **negative** opinion.

Write the correct letter in each box.

What did the woman think of …

(a) the fish? ☐

(b) the vegetables? ☐

(c) the wine? ☐

What did the man think of …

(d) the chicken? ☐

(e) the wine? ☐

(f) the ice cream? ☐

(6 marks)

Healthy living and lifestyle

Had a go ☐   Nearly there ☐   Nailed it! ☐

A healthy diet

Healthy eating

1 You read this online post about healthy eating for young people.

> **Iss dich gesund!**
> Alle Jugendliche brauchen verschiedene Arten von Essen*, um gesund zu sein.
> Hier sind unsere Top-Regeln:
> Regel 1:   Täglich Obst essen. Das vermeidet das Hungergefühl.
> Regel 2:   So oft wie möglich frisches Gemüse essen, um mehr Energie zu haben.
> Regel 3:   Ab und zu Fisch oder Fleisch essen, um die Muskeln zu stärken.
> Regel 4:   Regelmäßig Käse und andere Milchprodukte essen. Das macht stark.
> Regel 5:   Genug Wasser trinken, um den ganzen Körper zu schützen.
> Regel 6:   Selten Kuchen und Zucker essen, denn zu viel davon kann Krankheiten verursachen.
> Regel 7:   Langsam und ruhig essen, um jedes Gericht richtig zu genießen.
> Regel 8:   Sehr oft etwas Grünes essen – das ist gut für das Herz.
> Regel 9:   Jeden Tag mit einem guten Frühstück anfangen – der beste Start in den Tag!
> Regel 10: Nicht zu oft Fastfood essen.

* *Arten von Essen* – types of food

Answer the following questions in **English**.

(a) Why should you eat fruit daily? ....
(b) According to the text, why are fresh vegetables good for you? ....
(c) How often should you eat meat or fish? ....
(d) What is the benefit of dairy products? ....
(e) What can you do to protect your whole body? ....
(f) What does Rule 7 recommend? ....
(g) What types of food improve heart health? ....
(h) What does Rule 9 advise? ....

(8 marks)

Translation

2 Translate these sentences into **English**.

Ich esse normalerweise gesund, obwohl ich manchmal Pommes genieße.

....

Sie sind lecker, wenn man Hunger hat.

....

Das Frühstück ist für mich das wichtigste Essen des Tages.

....

Es gibt mir die Energie, die ich für den ganzen Morgen brauche.

....

Gestern habe ich Eier mit Brot gegessen und morgen werde ich viel Obst vorbereiten.

....

(10 marks)

Had a go ☐ **Nearly there** ☐ **Nailed it!** ☐

Healthy living and lifestyle

Sporting events

Picture task

> To respond to this question, always begin with the people you see in the picture. Say how many people there are, whether they are male or female, how old they are, what they look like and / or what they are wearing.

1 You see this photo online.

   What is in this photo?

   Write **five** sentences in **German**.

   ....
   ....
   ....
   ....
   .... **(10 marks)**

Photo card

2 Talk about the content of these photos. You must say at least **one** thing about each photo. **(5 marks)**

Photo 1   Photo 2

After you have spoken about the content of the photos, listen to the recording of further questions on the topic of **People and lifestyle**. Pause the recording to give your answers. You should try to develop your answers as much as you can. **(20 marks)**

> Remember that in the exam, there will be an extended unprepared conversation around the theme. These three example questions simply give you a idea of what to expect.

17

Healthy living and lifestyle

Had a go ☐   Nearly there ☐   Nailed it! ☐

Advantages of sport

Translation

1   Translate these sentences into **English**.

Ich bewege mich oft.

....

Jeden Morgen gehe ich laufen.

....

Sport ist wirklich gesund und macht auch viel Spaß.

....

Gestern haben mein Bruder und ich nach der Schule Fußball gespielt.

....

Wenn er im Meer schwimmt, vergisst er seine Probleme.

....   **(10 marks)**

> If you see *gestern / letzte Woche*, the verb is likely to be in a past tense.
>
> When you see *wenn*, look to the end of the clause for the verb.

Reading aloud

2   Read aloud the following text in **German**.

> Ich treibe regelmäßig und sehr gerne Sport, vor allem Tennis und Fußball.
> Wenn ich mich genug bewege, fühle ich mich immer besser.
> Alle Menschen sind glücklicher, wenn sie täglich aktiv sind.
> Ich hoffe, ich werde ein längeres Leben haben, weil ich gesund lebe.
> Ab und zu ist es wichtig, etwas Entspannendes zu tun.

(5 marks)

> You may wish to mark any pauses to take a breath; read steadily rather than rushing through the reading.

Pay attention to these sounds:

- *ei* in *treibe / weil* – sounds like the English word 'I'
- *Sp* in *Sport* – sounds like 'shp'
- *w* in *wenn / werde / weil* – sounds like 'v'
- *ä* in *regelmäßig / täglich / längeres* – sounds like a combination of 'a' and 'e', a bit like the first part of the English word 'air'
- *ü* in *glücklicher* – sounds like 'u' and 'e' with your lips pursed
- final *-e* in *treibe / gerne / werde*, etc – pronounced as a separate syllable.

Listen to the recording to practise these sounds.

Track 24

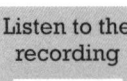

Now play the recording to listen to and answer four questions in **German** that relate to the topic of **Healthy living and lifestyle**.

In order to score the highest marks, you must try to **answer all four questions as fully as you can**.

(10 marks)

Had a go ☐ Nearly there ☐ Nailed it! ☐

Healthy living and lifestyle

Physical wellbeing

Translation

1 Translate these sentences into **English**.

Ich schlafe immer gut.

....

Mein Freund und ich spielen gern Fußball.

....

Wenn ich Zeit habe, gehe ich morgens laufen.

....

Letztes Wochenende bin ich mit meinem Stiefbruder schwimmen gegangen.

....

Ich möchte in der Zukunft Tennis spielen.

....

> Check the verb first – be aware of the person and the tense.
>
> Check carefully to ensure you don't miss any words like *immer, gern* or *morgens*.

(10 marks)

A new gym

2 You read Max's online review of a new gym.

> Das neue Fitness-Studio hat mir gefallen, und ich überlege, ob ich ein Mitglied werden soll. Wenn man kein Mitglied ist, sind die Preise etwas höher. Aber man muss entscheiden, ob es den Preis wert ist. Das ist nur der Fall, wenn man mindestens dreimal pro Woche hingeht. Ich denke, ich kann das machen. Ich habe zum Beispiel Lust, Gewichtheben* zu probieren. Das ist schwierig, aber man kann viel stärker werden und alle seine Muskeln entwickeln, nicht nur die Arme, sondern auch die Beine und den Rücken. Der Fitnessraum hat tolle Maschinen, womit man bestimmte Körperteile trainieren kann, und es gibt auch ein tolles Schwimmbad mit Tauchbecken**. **Max**

Gewichtheben – weightlifting
**Becken* – pool

Read the following statements and write the correct letters in each box.

Write **A** if only statement A is correct

  B if only statement B is correct

  A+B if both statements A and B are correct.

(a) **A** Max says it's better value to join the gym.

  B He would need to go regularly to make membership worthwhile. ☐ **(1 mark)**

(b) **A** Max thinks he can't manage regular visits.

  B Max thinks he could try some new exercise classes. ☐ **(1 mark)**

(c) **A** Weightlifting will help Max lose weight.

  B Weightlifting will strengthen his back. ☐ **(1 mark)**

(d) **A** Max is impressed by the exercise machines.

  B Max is impressed by the personal trainers. ☐ **(1 mark)**

| Healthy living and lifestyle | Had a go ☐ Nearly there ☐ Nailed it! ☐ |

Mental wellbeing

Listen to the recording

Dictation

1. Play the recording of four short sentences.

   Listen carefully and using your knowledge of German sounds, write down in **German** exactly what you hear for each sentence.

   You will hear each sentence **three** times: the first time as a full sentence, the second time in short sections and the third time again as a full sentence.

   Use your knowledge of German sounds and grammar to make sure that what you have written makes sense. Check carefully that your spelling is accurate.

   Sentence 1 ....

   Sentence 2 ....

   Sentence 3 ....

   Sentence 4 ....   **(8 marks)**

Track 27

> Listen to this audio to remind yourself how to pronounce the German sounds.
> - *-e* – at the end of a word is a separate syllable
> - *w* – sounds like 'v'
> - *j* – sounds like 'y'
> - *ü* – sounds like 'u' and 'e' combined
> - *-ig* – at the end of the word is a soft throaty sound like the German *ch*
> - *z* – sounds like 'ts'
> - *ie* – sounds like 'ee'.

Translation

2. Translate the following sentences into **German**.

   This school year is very important for me.

   ....

   There is a lot of pressure because we have exams in summer.

   ....

   If I have questions, I talk to my teacher.

   ....

   In my opinion it is good to exercise and to spend time with friends.

   ....

   You should always talk about your problems.

   ....   **(10 marks)**

> Watch out for these structures and, if you've forgotten them, check how they work in German:
> - *weil* – word order
> - *wenn* – word order
> - strong verbs
> - inversion
> - *zu* + infinitive clauses
> - modal verb + infinitive.

Had a go ☐ Nearly there ☐ Nailed it! ☐ | **Healthy living and lifestyle**

Feeling unwell

Picture task

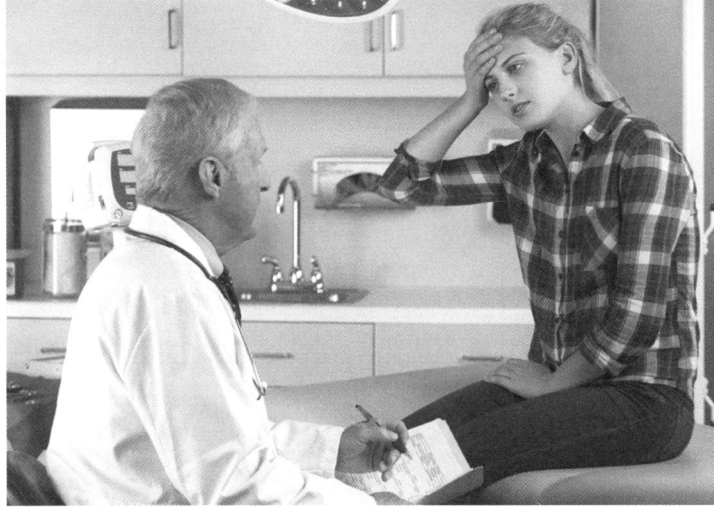

Remember to mention:
- the people (gender, age, clothes, appearance)
- the situation / place
- what they are doing
- anything else you observe.

1 You see this photo in a magazine.

What is in this photo?

Write **five** sentences in **German**.

....

....

....

....

.... **(10 marks)**

Describing symptoms

2 Three Swiss friends are talking about feeling unwell.

What **two** symptoms does each person have?

Write the correct letters in the boxes.

A	backache	E	headache
B	difficulty sleeping	F	loss of appetite
C	earache	G	sore eyes
D	feeling hot	H	stomach-ache

(a) Anna ☐ ☐

(b) Jan   ☐ ☐

(c) Lara   ☐ ☐

(6 marks)

21

Healthy living and lifestyle

Had a go ☐ Nearly there ☐ Nailed it! ☐

Avoiding health risks

Picture task

Just remember: Who? What? Where?
- Who is in the picture? Describe their appearance, mood and clothes.
- What are they doing? Are they dancing, laughing, talking?
- Where are they? Indoors or outdoors, at home, in a club?

1 You see this photo on Instagram.

   What is in this photo?

   Write **five** sentences in **German**.

   ....
   ....
   ....
   ....
   .... **(10 marks)**

My lifestyle

2 You are writing to a German friend about lifestyle.

   Write approximately **90** words in **German**.

   You must write something about each bullet point.

   Describe:
   - what you do to stay healthy
   - what you have done recently for your fitness
   - how you will celebrate the end of the exams.

   Make sure you respond using the right tense. For this question, there will always be one bullet point in each main time frame – present, past and future.

   ....
   ....
   ....
   ....
   ....
   ....
   ....
   ....
   .... **(15 marks)**

Had a go ☐   Nearly there ☐   Nailed it! ☐

Education and work

My school

Picture task

Remember the key content:
- Who can you see?
- Where are they?
- What are they doing?
- You can start each response with *Es gibt …* (There is / are …) or *Ich sehe …* (I can see …).

1 You see this photo online.

   What is in this photo?

   Write **five** sentences in **German**.

   ....
   ....
   ....
   ....
   ....   **(10 marks)**

Photo card

2 Talk about the content of these photos. You must say at least **one** thing about each photo.

(5 marks)

Photo 1   **Photo 2**

Although the photos in the exam will be in black and white, it's fine to use colour adjectives as part of your description.

Listen to the recording

After you have spoken about the content of the photos, listen to the recording of further questions on the topic of **Education and work**. Pause the recording to give your answers. You should try to develop your answers as much as you can.

(20 marks)

Education and work

Had a go ☐   Nearly there ☐   Nailed it! ☐

School subjects

Role play

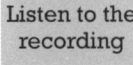

1 You are talking to your Austrian friend.

Listen to the recording of the teacher's part. The teacher will play the part of your friend and will speak first.

You should address your friend as *du*.

When you see this – **?** – you will have to ask a question.

> 1 Say what your best subjects are. (Give **two** details.)
> 2 Say what you think of homework. (Give **two** details.)
> ?3 Ask your friend about school subjects.
> 4 Say what you want to do next school year.
> 5 Say which subject you don't enjoy. (Give **one** detail and **one** reason.)

(10 marks)

School life

2 You read these posts by some German students about school.

> **Robin:** Ich finde alle meine Stunden ganz gut, aber einige Fächer sind besser als andere. Mathe ist mein bestes Fach, aber ich bin schwach in Kunst.
>
> **Malik:** Meine Lieblingsfächer sind Wissenschaft und Kunst, aber Englisch finde ich langweilig, und die Hausaufgaben sind zu schwierig!
>
> **Jana:** Ich muss sagen, ich bin eine faule Schülerin und arbeite nicht viel. Ich mag den Sportunterricht, denn das macht Spaß, und Englisch und Geschichte sind auch nicht schlecht. Aber warum muss ich jeden Tag Mathe lernen?

Match the correct person with each of the following questions.

Write **R** for **Robin**

     M for **Malik**

     J for **Jana.**

Write the correct letter in each box.

(a) Who loves science subjects? ☐

(b) Who thinks there are too many maths lessons? ☐

(c) Who finds English homework difficult? ☐

(d) Who is not very hardworking? ☐

(e) Who enjoys all their lessons? ☐

(5 marks)

Had a go ☐   Nearly there ☐   Nailed it! ☐   **Education and work**

My teachers

This year at school and teaching

1 You are writing a blog about education.

Write approximately **150** words in **German**.

You must write something about both bullet points.

Describe:
- how you have found school life this year
- why you would like / not like to be a teacher in the future.

> Try to develop your ideas in some detail and aim to use some complex structures, such as:
> - *um ... zu*
> - *dass* – word order
> - *weil* – word order
> - relative clauses
> - inversion – verb in second place
> - *obwohl* – word order
> - the passive
> - the conditional (for the second bullet point).

....

....

....

....

....

....

....

....

....

....

(25 marks)

Reading aloud

2 Read aloud the following text in **German**.

> Ich habe einige tolle Lehrer.
> Meine Englischlehrerin ist sehr freundlich.
> Ich mag den Unterricht in meiner Schule.
> In Kunst bin ich stark und ich finde das Fach nicht schwierig.
> Ein guter Lehrer soll den Schülern helfen.

(5 marks)

> Sounds to watch out for here:
> - final -*e* – sound the syllable
> - final -*ich* – a soft sound in the throat (not 'ick'!)
> - *rr* – try to roll the *r* sound at the back of your throat
> - *st* – sounds like 'sht'
> - final -*ig* – sounds like 'ich' (see above)
> - *ü* – like a 'u' and 'e' combined, with pursed lips.
> Listen to the recording to practise these sounds.

Track 31

Now play the recording to listen to and answer four questions in **German** that relate to the topic of **Education and work**.

In order to score the highest marks, you must try to **answer all four questions as fully as you can**.

(10 marks)

25

Education and work

Had a go ☐   Nearly there ☐   Nailed it! ☐

The school day

My school day

1. You are writing to an Austrian friend about your school day.

   Write approximately **90** words in **German**.

   You must write something about each bullet point.

   Describe:
   - how you find the school day
   - what you did at break yesterday
   - what you will do in school tomorrow.

   > For the first bullet point, say something about your timetable. Remember to explain any opinions. For example, is the school day too long? Is break too short? Does school start too early?

   ....
   ....
   ....
   ....
   ....
   ....
   ....
   ....
   ....
   ....
   ....
   .... **(15 marks)**

School timetable

2. Elias is talking about his timetable.

   Answer the questions in **English**.

   (a) What does Elias like about Mondays?

   ....

   (b) Which lesson does he have on Monday afternoon?

   ....

   (c) What are his first **two** lessons on Tuesday?

   ....

   (d) When is the music lesson on Tuesday?

   ....

   (e) What is his first lesson on Wednesday?

   .... **(6 marks)**

Listen to the recording

> Make quick notes as you listen for the first time – note the day and the subjects you hear in the order in which you hear them and try to decide on some of the answers.

Had a go ☐ Nearly there ☐ Nailed it! ☐

Education and work

School uniform

My school uniform

1 You are writing to a German friend about your school uniform.

Write approximately **90** words in **German**.

You must write something about each bullet point.

Describe:
- what you think of your school uniform
- what you wore for a recent sports lesson
- what you will wear this evening.

> The second bullet point is in the past tense and the third bullet point is in the future. Make sure you use the appropriate time frame to respond to these points.

....
....
....
....
....
....
....
....
....
....

(15 marks)

Translation

2 Translate the following sentences into **German**.

I do not like the uniform.

....

In school we wear a blue jacket and a white shirt.

....

The boys must wear grey trousers.

....

You are only allowed to wear black shoes.

....

Yesterday, I bought red socks.

....

(10 marks)

> Ask yourself whether 'You' in the fourth sentence should be translated as *du* or *man*.

Education and work

Had a go ☐ Nearly there ☐ Nailed it! ☐

School rules

Role play

1 You are talking to your German friend.

Listen to the recording of the teacher's part. The teacher will play the part of your friend and will speak first.

You should address your friend as *du*.

When you see this – ? – you will have to ask a question.

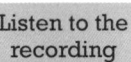

> 1 Say what you think of the school rules.
> 2 Say which rule you think is good. (Give **one** detail.)
> ?3 Ask your friend a question about their school rules.
> 4 Say what you think of school uniform.
> 5 Say something about a rule you don't like.

In order to score full marks, you must include a verb in your response to each task.

(10 marks)

Make notes during the preparation time of what you intend to say.

Role play

2 You are talking to your Austrian friend.

Listen to the recording of the teacher's part. The teacher will play the part of your friend and will speak first.

You should address your friend as *du*.

When you see this – ? – you will have to ask a question.

> 1 Say why you think school rules are important. (Give **two** details.)
> 2 Say which rule you think is the most important. (Give **one** opinion and **one** reason.)
> ?3 Ask your friend a question about their school rules.
> 4 Say which rule you don't like. (Give **one** opinion and **one** reason.)
> 5 Say what you think of mobile phones in school.

(10 marks)

In order to score full marks, you must include a verb in your response to each task.

You don't need to develop your answers with too much detail. Short, relevant and clear comments are best.

Had a go ☐   Nearly there ☐   Nailed it! ☐

Education and work

Homework

My homework

1 You are writing to a Swiss friend about homework.

Write approximately **90** words in **German**.

You must write something about each bullet point.

Describe:
- the importance of homework
- last night's homework
- what school work you will do this evening.

> Make sure you address all three bullet points, although you don't need to cover them in equal detail.

> Note that the second bullet point needs a response in the past and the third bullet point in the future time frame.

....
....
....
....
....
....
....
....

(15 marks)

Translation

2 Translate the following sentences into **German**.

At school I work hard and always try to get good marks

....
....

I do a lot of homework every day.

....
....

I think it is important to take responsibility for your own learning.

....
....

Yesterday evening, I spent three hours on German homework.

....
....

That was difficult, but I think that I understand better now.

....
....

> There are some complex structures here, so think carefully about word order / where to put the verbs.

(10 marks)

> If there's a word you don't know, try to use a sensible alternative rather than leave a gap.

Education and work

Had a go ☐   Nearly there ☐   Nailed it! ☐

Stress at school

Coping with school stress

1 You read this online advice for parents about helping young people with stress.

> Kinder und Jugendliche brauchen eine sichere Umgebung, die sie unterstützt. Am wichtigsten ist es, mit dem / der Jugendlichen im Gespräch zu bleiben, damit es immer einen engen Kontakt gibt.
>
> Wenn Sie immer bereit sind, mit ihr / ihm zu sprechen, zeigt das, dass er / sie wichtig ist und dass Sie versuchen, seine / ihre Probleme zu verstehen.
>
> Stellen Sie sich die folgenden Fragen:
> - Schläft er / sie genug?
> - Gibt es eine klare Struktur mit festen Zeiten für Essen und Hausaufgaben?
> - Gibt es einen Lernplan, damit er / sie Stück für Stück* die Arbeit schafft und erfolgreich wird?

* *Stück für Stück* – bit by bit

> Note that a phrase is glossed for you. This should help you understand the last line of the text.

Answer the following questions in **English**.

(a) What sort of surroundings are helpful for stressed young people?

.... **(1 marks)**

(b) What are the **two** most important things that parents should do?

(i) ....

(ii) .... **(2 marks)**

(c) Which elements of daily routine are mentioned? (Give **two** details.)

(i) ....

(ii) .... **(2 marks)**

Reading aloud

2 Read aloud the following text in **German**.

> Ich habe viel zu lernen.
> Es gibt bald wichtige Prüfungen.
> Ich habe Angst, dass ich dieses Jahr nicht genug gelernt habe.
> Ich werde heute Abend drei Stunden Hausaufgaben machen.
> Ich muss Deutsch, Englisch und Mathe wiederholen.

(5 marks)

> Sounds to watch out for here:
> - *ch* – sounds soft and throaty, not like 'ck'
> - *j* – sounds like 'y'
> - *-g* – sounds more like 'ch'
> - *ü* – sounds like a combination of 'u' and 'e', spoken with pursed lips
> - watch the *e* sound in the word *Englisch* – it sounds like the 'e' in 'egg'!
>
> Listen to the recording to practise these sounds.

Track 36

Listen to the recording

Now play the recording to listen to and answer four questions in **German** that relate to the topic of **Education and work**. In order to score the highest marks, you must try to **answer all four questions as fully as you can**.

(10 marks)

Had a go ☐   **Nearly there** ☐   **Nailed it!** ☐   **Education and work**

My ideal school

Picture task

You could write about the following:
1. The people in the photo – their clothes, age, appearance.
2. Where they are – outside, in front of a school.
3. What they are doing – leaving school, going home.
4. What the school building looks like.

1 You see this photo on Instagram.

   What is in this photo?

   Write **five** sentences in **German**.

   Remember that *Es gibt …* or *Ich sehe …* are good starting points for your sentences.

   ....

   ....

   ....

   ....

   .... **(10 marks)**

Dictation

2 Play the recording of five short sentences.

   Listen carefully and using your knowledge of German sounds, write down in **German** exactly what you hear for each sentence.

   You will hear each sentence **three** times: the first time as a full sentence, the second time in short sections and the third time again as a full sentence.

   Use your knowledge of German sounds and grammar to make sure that what you have written makes sense. Check carefully that your spelling is accurate.

   Sentence 1 ....

   Sentence 2 ....

   Sentence 3 ....

   Sentence 4 ....

   Sentence 5 .... **(10 marks)**

Sounds to listen out for here:
- *sch* – sounds like 'sh'
- *äu* – sounds like 'oy'
- *ü* – sounds like 'u' and 'e' combined, with pursed lips.
- *w* – sounds like 'v'
- *ä* – sounds like 'a' and 'e' combined
- *ch* – a soft sound, as in *ich*
- *z* – sounds like 'ts'.

Listen to the recording to practise these sounds.

Track 39

Education and work

Had a go ☐   Nearly there ☐   Nailed it! ☐

Preparing for exams

Role play

Listen to the recording

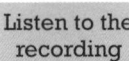

1   You are talking to your German friend.

Listen to the recording of the teacher's part. The teacher will play the part of your friend and will speak first.

You should address your friend as *du*.

When you see this – ? – you will have to ask a question.

> 1 Say how long you spend on school work each evening.
> 2 Say where you do your work.
> 3 Say how often you have a break.
> 4 Say why you are working hard.
> ?5 Ask your friend a question about exams.

> Pay particular attention to formulating the question you need to ask for the last task. Keep the question simple. For example, you could ask *Wie findest du …?*

(5 marks)

Dictation

Listen to the recording

2   Play the recording of five short sentences.

Listen carefully and using your knowledge of German sounds, write down in **German** exactly what you hear for each sentence.

You will hear each sentence **three** times: the first time as a full sentence, the second time in short sections and the third time again as a full sentence.

Sentence 1

....

Sentence 2

....

Sentence 3

....

Sentence 4

....

Sentence 5

....

(10 marks)

> Sounds to listen out for here:
> - final *-e* – always sounded as a separate syllable
> - *g* – sounds like English 'g' as in 'gate'
> - *ei* – sounds like English 'I'
> - *ä* – sounds like 'a' and 'e' combined
> - *ö* – sounds like 'o' and 'e' combined
> - *st* – sounds like 'sht'.
>
> Listen to the recording to practise these sounds.

Track 42

Had a go ☐ Nearly there ☐ Nailed it! ☐

Education and work

Gap year

Translation

1 Translate these sentences into **English**.

Ich habe heute meine letzte Prüfung.

....

Mein Bruder macht eine Zugreise durch Frankreich.

....

Nächstes Jahr werde ich mit kranken Tieren arbeiten.

....

Im Ausland ist es nützlich, andere Sprachen zu sprechen.

....

Einige Freunde wollen im Herbst nach Europa fahren.

.... **(10 marks)**

Unprepared conversation questions

2 Listen to the questions in the recording and give your answers in the pauses.

Pause the recording if you need more time.

There will be questions in the present, past and future tenses.

Your responses should be as full and detailed as possible. **(20 marks)**

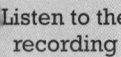

> After you have completed the photo card part of the Speaking exam, there will be a longer unprepared conversation on any or all of the three topics within the theme of the photo card. This will last around **five minutes**.
>
> The photo card that these questions follow concerns post-18 plans, so it relates to the theme of **People and lifestyle**, which includes the following topics:
> - Identity and relationships with others
> - Healthy living and lifestyle
> - Education and work.
>
> This is your chance to go beyond short, concise answers and develop your ideas in more detail.
>
> It is also an opportunity to express and explain opinions, use all three time frames, and show off some more complex language.

Education and work

Had a go ☐   Nearly there ☐   Nailed it! ☐

Plans for next year

Grammar task

1 Using your knowledge of grammar, complete the following sentences in **German**.

Choose the correct German word from the three options in the grid.

Write the correct **word** in the space, as shown in the example below.

Example:

Ich .....*gehe*..... in die Schule.

geht	gehe	gehen

(a) Wir .... gern Englisch.

lernen	lerne	lernt

(b) .... Deutschlehrerin ist freundlich.

Der	Die	Das

(c) .... Jahr will ich die Schule verlassen.

Nächstes	Nächste	Nächsten

(d) Er .... auf die Uni gehen.

werden	wirst	wird

(e) Ich habe gute Noten ....

bekommt	bekommen	bekomme

> Key language aspects to look out for here are:
> - correct verb forms (a) and (d)
> - genders of nouns (b)
> - adjective endings (c)
> - correct past participle (e).

(5 marks)

Role play

2 You are talking to your German friend.

Listen to the recording of the teacher's part. The teacher will play the part of your friend and will speak first.

You should address your friend as *du*.

When you see this – ? – you will have to ask a question.

> 1 Say what you would like to learn in the sixth form. (Give **two** details.)
> ?2 Ask your friend about staying on at school.
> 3 Say what your best subject is this year. (Give **one** opinion and **one** reason.)
> 4 Say whether you would like to go to university.
> 5 Say what sort of job you would like in the future.

(10 marks)

> Plan how you will formulate the question.

> Keep your answers short – simply say enough to provide the information required.

Had a go ☐ **Nearly there** ☐ **Nailed it!** ☐

Education and work

Future studies

Picture task

> Remember to consider the people, place and activity.

> Write a complete sentence (i.e. with a verb) each time.

> Keep your sentences short and clear, as they are more likely to be accurate and score 2 marks.

1 You see this photo online.

What is in this photo?

Write **five** sentences in **German**.

....
....
....
....
.... **(10 marks)**

Photo card

2 Talk about the content of these photos. You must say at least **one** thing about each photo. **(5 marks)**

Photo 1

Photo 2

> To refer to the foreground figures, start with *Vorne* (at the front).

Listen to the recording

After you have spoken about the content of the photos, listen to the recording of further questions that relate to **any** of the topics within the theme of **People and lifestyle**.
Pause the recording to give your answers. You should try to develop your answers as much as you can.

(20 marks)

> Remember that in the exam, there will be an extended unprepared conversation around the theme. These three example questions simply give you an idea of what to expect.

Education and work

Had a go ☐ Nearly there ☐ Nailed it! ☐

Future career

My jobs and career

1 You are writing to a German friend about jobs and careers.

Write approximately **90** words in **German**.

You must write something about each bullet point.

Describe:
- what is important for you in a job
- a holiday job you have had in the past
- what work you will do in future.

> Note that for this question, the second bullet point is always in the past, and the third bullet point is in the future time frame. It's important that you use verbs in the appropriate tenses.

....
....
....
....
....
....
....
....
....
....

(15 marks)

Reading aloud

2 Read aloud the following text in **German**.

> Ich interessiere mich vor allem für die Umwelt.
> Heute ist Umweltverschmutzung ein ernstes Problem.
> Es gibt so viele Gefahren für unsere Welt.
> Aus diesem Grund möchte ich in der Zukunft im Bereich Umweltschutz arbeiten.
> Ich bin nicht sicher, welche Berufsmöglichkeiten es gibt, aber ich denke, diese Arbeit ist wichtig.

(5 marks)

Sounds to watch out for here:
- v – sounds like a soft 'f'
- short *e* – you need this sound in words like *allem* and *Umwelt*
- long *e* – you need this sound in words like *Problem*
- *ie* – sounds like the English 'ee', e.g. *diese*
- *ei* – sounds like the English 'I', e.g. *Bereich, arbeiten*
- *w* – sounds like 'v', e.g. *Welt, welche, wichtig*.

Listen to the recording to practise these sounds.

Track 46

Listen to the recording

Now play the recording to listen to and answer four questions in **German** that relate to the topic of **Education and work**.

In order to score the highest marks, you must try to **answer all four questions as fully as you can**.

(10 marks)

Had a go ☐ Nearly there ☐ Nailed it! ☐

Education and work

Opinions about jobs

Discussing jobs

1 You are writing to a German friend about future jobs.

Write approximately **90** words in **German**.

You must write something about each bullet point.

Describe:

- your opinion of what makes a good job
- how you have earned money in the past
- which job you would like to have in the future.

> Note that the second bullet point is in the past tense. If you haven't earned money in the past, say that and explain why. Or again, you can invent a way you have earned money. If you have less to say on this point, that's fine, as you can make up the word count on the other bullet points (see the sample response in the Answers section).

....

....

....

....

....

....

....

....

....

....   **(15 marks)**

Translation

2 Translate these sentences into **English**.

Ich mag Kunst und Englisch.

....

In meiner Freizeit lese ich gern.

....

In der Zukunft möchte ich irgendwie mit Büchern arbeiten.

....

Es ist wichtig für mich, meinen Arbeitstag zu genießen.

....

Ich hoffe, ich werde die richtige Arbeitsstelle mit netten Mitarbeitern finden.

....   **(10 marks)**

Free-time activities

Had a go ☐ Nearly there ☐ Nailed it! ☐

Free-time activities

Photo card

1 Talk about the content of these photos. You must say at least **one** thing about each photo. **(5 marks)**

Photo 1   Photo 2

> Remember to talk about the people, their locations and their activities.

After you have spoken about the content of the photos, listen to the recording of further questions related to **any** of the topics within the theme of **Popular culture**. Pause the recording to give your answers. You should try to develop your answers as much as you can.

(20 marks)

Popular hobbies

2 You read this article about popular hobbies among German adults last year.

> Gartenarbeit war im letzten Jahr für 23% der Deutschen das beliebteste Hobby. 26% der Bevölkerung gingen in ihrer Freizeit gern einkaufen. 20% der Befragten* fotografierten gern. Die beliebteste sportliche Aktivität war der Besuch im Fitness-Studio – damit verbrachten etwa 10,9% ihre Freizeit. Andere Freizeitaktivitäten, die man erwähnte**, waren zum Essen ausgehen, Kinobesuche und auch traditionelle **Gesellschaftsspiele**, wo man mit Freunden oder Familie bequem um den Tisch sitzt, um einen lustigen Abend beim Spielen zu verbringen.

* *Befragten* – people surveyed
** *erwähnen* – to mention

Answer the following questions in **English**.

(a) What was the preferred hobby for 23% of Germans?

....

(b) What percentage of people enjoyed shopping?

....

(c) What sort of sports activity was the most popular?

....

(d) Read the last sentence again. What does **Gesellschaftsspiele** mean?

Write the correct letter in the box.

A	ball games
B	board games
C	computer games

☐

(4 marks)

Had a go ☐ Nearly there ☐ Nailed it! ☐

Free-time activities

Music and dance

Photo card

1 Talk about the content of these photos. You must say at least **one** thing about each photo. **(5 marks)**

Photo 1

Photo 2

> People – what do they look like and what are they wearing?
> Place – where are they?
> Activity – what are they doing?

After you have spoken about the content of the photos, listen to the recording of further questions that relate to **any** of the topics within the theme of **Popular culture**. Pause the recording to give your answers. You should try to develop your answers as much as you can.

(20 marks)

Tastes in music

2 You hear your friend Mika talking about music.

Choose the correct answer and write the correct letter in each box.

(a) What is Mika's taste in music?

A	He likes different types of music.
B	He prefers classical music.
C	He only likes rock music.

(b) What does he think of rap music?

A	It is meaningless.
B	It is too loud.
C	It has a message.

(c) What did he used to listen to?

A	Pop music.
B	Rock music.
C	Musicals.

(d) What would he like to do in the future?

A	Learn to dance.
B	Be a singer.
C	Manage a band.

(4 marks)

> Always have a quick look at the questions before you listen to the recording.

> You'll notice here that two questions are not in the present tense, so listen for an imperfect tense verb for question (c) and a future time frame for question (d).

Free-time activities   Had a go ☐   Nearly there ☐   Nailed it! ☐

Arranging to go out

Weekend activities

1 Leonie and Max are talking about weekend plans.

 What do they say?

 Write the correct the letter in each box.

(a) What will Max do on Saturday?

A	He will go for a walk.
B	He will go shopping.
C	He will go cycling.

(b) What does he need?

A	He needs clothes.
B	He needs books.
C	He needs trainers.

(c) What is Leonie's plan?

A	She wants to get up early.
B	She wants to have breakfast.
C	She wants to sleep late.

(d) Where will they meet?

A	At the marketplace.
B	At the shopping centre.
C	At a café.

(e) What will they do next?

A	They will have lunch.
B	They will have ice cream.
C	They will have coffee.

(5 marks)

> Listen the first time to get a rough idea of what the conversation is about and make some quick notes of any words you hear in German. This will help you decide on your answers during the second listen.

Dictation

2 Play the recording of five short sentences.

 Listen carefully and using your knowledge of German sounds, write down in **German** exactly what you hear for each sentence.

 You will hear each sentence **three** times: the first time as a full sentence, the second time in short sections and the third time again as a full sentence.

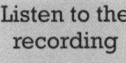

 Use your knowledge of German sounds and grammar to make sure that what you have written makes sense. Check carefully that your spelling is accurate.

 Sentence 1 ....

 Sentence 2 ....

 Sentence 3 ....

 Sentence 4 ....

 Sentence 5 .... **(10 marks)**

> Don't panic when the recording starts. Try doing the following to see if it works for you:
> - The first time, listen for gist and note down some words you hear in the right places.
> - During and straight after the second listen, try to fill in the gaps and write the sentences.
> - Check your work as you listen for the third time and note anything you need to think about when the recording is finished.

Had a go ☐ Nearly there ☐ Nailed it! ☐

Free-time activities

Reading

My reading habits

1 You are writing to an Austrian friend about reading.

   Write approximately **90** words in **German**.

   You must write something about each bullet point.

   Describe:
   - how often you read books
   - what you have read recently
   - what you plan to read next.

   > Note that an alternative to the future tense with *werden* is to use a future time expression (*morgen / nächste Woche*, etc) with a present tense verb, or to use *wollen* (to want to) followed by an infinitive.

   ....
   ....
   ....
   ....
   ....
   ....
   ....
   ....
   ....
   ....   **(15 marks)**

Translation

2 Translate the following sentences into **German**.

   I like reading and I always have a book with me.

   ....

   When I was younger, I read all the Harry Potter books.

   ....

   Now I prefer to read detective stories.

   ....

   At the moment, I am reading a new novel called *The Rules*.

   ....

   The main character is a boy who loves computers.

   ....   **(10 marks)**

   > Don't be confused by 'I am reading'. This is just another way of saying 'I read', so use the normal present tense in German.

   > You can translate the book title *The Rules* as „Die Regeln".

Free-time activities

Had a go ☐ Nearly there ☐ Nailed it! ☐

Television

Reading aloud

1 Read aloud the following text in **German**.

Then listen to the audio in the Answers section to check your pronunciation.

> Ich sehe fast jeden Tag fern.
> Meine Lieblingssendung ist eine Komödie.
> Die ganze Familie macht eine Pause, um sie anzusehen.
> Gestern habe ich einen Film über Pferde gesehen.
> Heute Abend will ich die Nachrichten hören.

(5 marks)

> Sounds to watch out for here:
> - *j* – sounds like 'y' in English
> - *ei* – sounds like the English 'I' sound
> - *ö* – sounds like 'er'
> - *z* – sounds like 'ts'
> - *ch* – a throaty sound, as in *ich*.
> Listen to the recording to practise these sounds.

Track 53

Now play the recording of four questions in **German** related to the topic of **Popular culture**.
In order to score the highest marks, you must try to **answer all four questions as fully as you can**.

(10 marks)

Role play

2 You are talking to your German friend.

Listen to the recording to hear the teacher's part. The teacher will play the part of your friend and will speak first.

You should address your friend as *du*.

When you see this – **?** – you will have to ask a question.

> 1 Say how often you watch television.
> 2 Say what sort of programmes you like. (Give **two** details.)
> ?3 Ask your friend a question about television.
> 4 Say what you think of violence in TV programmes.
> 5 Say what sort of programmes are interesting for young people.

> Note those tasks where more than one detail is required or where an opinion and a reason are needed. Make sure you cover all these required elements.

(10 marks)

Had a go ☐ Nearly there ☐ Nailed it! ☐ **Free-time activities**

Film and cinema

Grammar task

1 Using your knowledge of grammar, complete the following sentences in **German**.

Choose the correct **German** word from the three options in the grid.

Write the correct **word** in the space, as shown in the example below.

Example:

Ich ......gehe...... in die Stadt.

| geht | gehe | gehen |

> Remember: basic grammar is being tested here. Key areas are verb forms, adjective endings, cases and genders.

(a) Ich .... Krimis langweilig.

| findest | finden | finde |

(b) Hast du .... Film gesehen?

| der | den | das |

(c) Im Kino .... es bequeme Sitzplätze.

| gibt | gebe | gibst |

(d) Das ist eine .... Geschichte.

| spannende | spannendes | spannenden |

(e) .... Schauspieler spielt eine große Rolle.

| Der | Die | Das |

(5 marks)

Translation

2 Translate these sentences into **English**.

Ich gehe selten ins Kino, weil die Karten heute so teuer sind.

....

Ich finde es aber eine gute Erfahrung, wenn ich mit Freunden einen Film sehe.

....

Die besten Filme sind meiner Meinung nach Action- und Kriegsfilme.

....

Alles passiert sehr schnell, und es ist immer spannend.

....

Letzten Monat habe ich einen deutschen Krimi gesehen.

....

(10 marks)

> Look at every word, and don't overlook the small but important ones like *so, aber, sehr, immer*.

Customs, festivals and celebrations Had a go ☐ Nearly there ☐ Nailed it! ☐

Celebrations

Picture task

> Remember to describe the people, where they are and what they are doing.
>
> It's a good idea to stick to the present tense.

> For this question, keep your responses short, but make sure you **use a verb** in each statement and that what you say is relevant to the image.

1   You see this photo on social media.

   What is in this photo?

   Write **five** sentences in **German.**

   ....
   ....
   ....
   ....
   .... **(10 marks)**

Translation

2   Translate the following sentences into **German**.

   In my family we always celebrate a birthday.
   ....
   We do that in order to spend more time together and have fun.
   ....
   My older brother has his birthday in April.
   ....
   Last year, we went to France for the weekend.
   ....
   Next year, I would like to have a big party at home.
   .... **(10 marks)**

> Watch out for verbs in different tenses. There are present and perfect tenses here and also a conditional in the last sentence, so don't forget the very useful *ich möchte* … with an infinitive at the end.
>
> There is also an example of the *um … zu* structure in the second sentence, so check that you recall how that is used and don't forget that *zu* + infinitive go to the end of the clause or sentence.

Had a go ☐   Nearly there ☐   Nailed it! ☐

Customs, festivals and celebrations

Customs and festivals

Celebrations

1 Two German friends, Eva and Ben, are talking about celebrations.

   Write **P** if they are talking about an event in the **past**

   N if they are talking about an event **now**

   F if they are talking about an event in the **future**.

   (a) Eva ☐

   (b) Ben ☐

   (2 marks)

Role play

2 You are talking to your Swiss friend.

   Listen to the recording of the teacher's part. The teacher will play the part of your friend and will speak first.

   You should address your friend as *du*.

   When you see this – **?** – you will have to ask a question.

   > 1 Say what you usually do at Christmas.
   > 2 Say what you think of family celebrations.
   > 3 Say how you celebrate your birthday.
   > 4 Say what your favourite birthday present is.
   > ?5 Ask your friend a question about celebrations.

   (10 marks)

   ....
   ....
   ....
   ....
   ....
   ....
   ....
   ....
   ....
   ....

   > Plan your responses carefully during the preparation time. Write bullet point notes which you can use as a guide in the exam.

   > Pay particular attention to formulating the question you need to ask. Keep the question simple. For example, you could ask *Wie findest du …?*

Customs, festivals and celebrations

Had a go ☐   Nearly there ☐   Nailed it! ☐

Places of interest

Picture task

Remember the key guidelines: Who? Where? What?
- Who is in the picture? Mention their gender, age, appearance, clothes.
- Where are they? If they are outside, mention the weather too. This is actually a picture of London, but you could simply write about it being a city with old buildings.
- What are they doing?

Although the picture is in black and white, you can still use colour adjectives in your sentences.

1 You see this photo on social media.

What is in this photo?

Write **five** sentences in **German**.

....

....

....

....

.... **(10 marks)**

My town and area

2 You are writing to a German friend about your town and area.

Write approximately **90** words in **German**.

You must write something about each bullet point.

Describe:
- a place of interest near where you live
- an interesting place you have visited in the past
- a place you would like to visit in the future.

Make sure that you write something in response to all **three** bullet points.

Your coverage of the points does not need to be even – if you have more to say about one of the points than others, then do so.

....

....

....

....

....

....

....

.... **(15 marks)**

Had a go ☐   Nearly there ☐   Nailed it! ☐

Customs, festivals and celebrations

Traditions

A festival in Munich

1 You read this tourist information about the Munich Oktoberfest.

> Das Oktoberfest, ein Bierfest, ist ein Festival, das im Herbst in München stattfindet und das sechzehn Tage dauert. Es beginnt normalerweise Ende September und endet Anfang Oktober. Das Festival ist berühmt für sein Bier, sein Essen und seine traditionelle bayerische Kleidung. Das Oktoberfest ist auch eine tolle Gelegenheit, neue Dinge auszuprobieren und verschiedene Kulturen zu erleben.
> Neben Bier gibt es auf dem Oktoberfest auch traditionelles deutsches Essen wie Würste und Brezen*, die sehr beliebt sind. Überall gibt es große Bierzelte, wo man verschiedene Biersorten genießen und deutsche Volksmusik von Live-Bands hören kann. Viele Besucher tragen traditionelle Kleidung – das heißt für Männer und Jungen eine Leder** hose und für Frauen und Mädchen ein **Dirndl**, ein schönes, oft rotes oder grünes Kleid.

* *Brezen* – pretzel, a salty snack   ** *Leder* – leather

Complete the sentences in **English**. Write **one** word in each space.

(a) Munich's Oktoberfest lasts .... days.

(b) The festival takes place in .... every year.

(c) The festival is a great opportunity to .... other cultures.

(d) Speciality foods are very .... at the beer festival.

(e) Live music is performed in the ....

(f) Read the last sentence again. What would you do with a **Dirndl**?

Write the correct letter in the box.

A	Eat it.
B	Drink it.
C	Wear it.

(6 marks)

> Remember that the questions follow the order in which the information appears in the text.

Picture task

2 You see this photo online.

What is in this photo?

Write **five** sentences in **German.**

....
....
....
....
....

(10 marks)

> As this photo is taken outside, this gives you an opportunity to say something about the weather. Here, you might use words for 'snow', 'dark', 'evening', 'cold'.

47

Customs, festivals and celebrations

Had a go ☐ Nearly there ☐ Nailed it! ☐

Learning languages

Reading aloud

1 Read aloud the following text in **German**.

> Meiner Meinung nach ist es wichtig, Fremdsprachen zu lernen.
> Wenn man ins Ausland fährt, ist es schön, mit anderen sprechen zu können.
> In unserer Schule lernen wir Deutsch und Französisch.
> Mein Bruder hat Spanisch gelernt und wohnt jetzt in Spanien.
> Ich hoffe, in der Zukunft für ein internationales Unternehmen zu arbeiten.

(5 marks)

Sounds to consider here:
- ig – sounds like the German ich
- z – has a crisp 'ts' sound
- ä – sounds like 'a' and 'e' combined
- ö – sounds like 'o' and 'e' combined
- sch – sounds like 'sh'
- sp – sounds like 'shp'
- w – sounds like 'v'
- -e – a final -e is a sounded syllable.

Listen to the recording to practise these sounds.

Track 58

Listen to the recording

Now play the recording to listen to and answer four questions in **German** related to the topic of **Customs, festivals and celebrations**.

In order to score the highest marks, you must try to **answer all four questions as fully as you can**.

(10 marks)

Language learning

2 You read these comments on learning languages.

> **Leonie:** Ich habe in der Schule Deutsch und Französisch gelernt. Die Stunden haben mir sehr gut gefallen, aber ich habe es schwierig gefunden, so viele neue Wörter zu lernen. Meine Noten in den Prüfungen waren leider sehr schlecht.
>
> **Matteo:** Spanisch finde ich einfach, weil mein Vater aus Spanien kommt. Deshalb lerne ich sehr gern diese Sprache, denn sie ist nützlich, wenn ich im Sommer bei meinen Großeltern bin.
>
> **Charlotte:** Ich finde Mathe, Physik und Wissenschaft besser als Fremdsprachen. Ich denke, Sprachen sind langweilig und nicht nötig für mich, denn es interessiert mich nicht, ins Ausland zu reisen.
>
> **Sascha:** Fremdsprachen sind mir wichtig, und ich lerne sie sehr gerne. Wir haben auch tolle Lehrer, die sehr lustig sind und die den Unterricht spannend machen. Das hilft mir viel, und ich habe immer Lust zu lernen. Ich hoffe, später Sprachen zu studieren.

What is the opinion of each person about their language learning experience?

Write **P** for a **positive** opinion

     N for a **negative** opinion

     P+N for a **positive** and **negative** opinion.

Write the correct letter in each box.

(a) Leonie ☐   (b) Matteo ☐   (c) Charlotte ☐

Answer the following question in **English**.

(d) What does Sascha say has helped her to enjoy learning languages? Give **two** details.

(i) .... (ii) .... **(5 marks)**

Had a go ☐   **Nearly there** ☐   **Nailed it!** ☐   **Celebrity culture**

Celebrity culture

Celebrity role models

1 You read these posts by some German students about people they admire.

> **Alexander:** Mein Lieblingsstar ist ein Fußballspieler aus Afrika. Er heißt Ade und ist nur einundzwanzig Jahre alt. Er hat so viel Talent.
>
> **Natalia:** Ich liebe einen französischen Schauspieler, der in ganz Europa sehr bekannt ist. Er spielt schwierige Rollen und spricht mindestens fünf Fremdsprachen. Er ist der ideale Mann.
>
> **Ben:** Mir gefällt eine Sängerin aus Italien, die Fulminata heißt. Ihre Stimme ist fantastisch stark und sie trägt tolle Kleidung.

Match the correct person with each of the following questions.

Write **A** for **Alexander**

  N for **Natalia**

  B for **Ben**.

Write the correct letter in each box.

(a) Who admires a singer? ☐

(b) Who admires an ability to speak other languages? ☐

(c) Whose favourite star is an actor? ☐

(d) Whose hero is 21 years old? ☐

(e) Who admires the fashion style of their celebrity? ☐

(5 marks)

Role play

2 You are talking to your German friend.

Listen to the recording of the teacher's part. The teacher will play the part of your friend and will speak first.

You should address your friend as *du*.

When you see this – **?** – you will have to ask a question.

> 1 Say something about a celebrity whom you like. (Give **two** details.)
> ?2 Ask your German friend about their favourite star.
> 3 Say whether you think celebrities are important. (Give **one** opinion and **one** reason.)
> 4 Say what your favourite celebrity has done recently.
> 5 Say what you will look at online tonight.

(10 marks)

> Plan your responses during the preparation time.
> • Don't overdevelop the responses – they need to be short, appropriate and clear.
> • Think about how to word the question you are required to ask.
> • Make your notes clear and concise and write them in the order in which you'll need them.

Celebrity culture

Had a go ☐ Nearly there ☐ Nailed it! ☐

Opinions about being a celebrity

Picture task

Although there are a number of people in the photo, only one is really clear enough to describe, so say who she is, what she looks like, what she is wearing and how she is feeling.

1 You see this picture on social media.

   What is in this photo?

   Write **five** sentences in **German**.

   ....

   ....

   ....

   ....

   ....

   (10 marks)

Reading aloud

2 Read aloud the following text in **German**.

> Man liest jeden Tag in den sozialen Medien über Stars, die berühmt sind.
> Es gibt Bilder von ihrer Kleidung, von ihren Familien, von ihren Häusern.
> Meiner Meinung nach hat das alles keinen Sinn.
> Aber solche Menschen machen bestimmt einen großen Eindruck auf Jugendliche.
> Das kann positive aber auch negative Folgen haben.

(5 marks)

Sounds to consider here:
- *ie* – sounds like the English 'ee'
- *z* – sounds like 'ts'
- *ü* – sounds like 'u' and 'e' combined
- *v* – sounds like 'f'
- *äu* – sounds rather like 'oy'
- *ei* – sounds like the English 'I'
- *j* – sounds like 'y'.

Listen to the recording to practise these sounds.

Track 61

Listen to the recording

Now play the recording to listen to four questions in **German** related to the topic of **Celebrity culture**.

In order to score the highest marks, you must try to **answer all four questions as fully as you can**.

(10 marks)

Had a go ☐ Nearly there ☐ Nailed it! ☐ **Celebrity culture**

Sports stars

German sports stars

1 You read this article about Verena Bentele, a former German Paralympian.

> Verena ist im Februar 1982 in Bayern geboren und schon ihr ganzes Leben lang blind. Sie hat sich immer für Sport interessiert, vor allem für Wintersport. Sie hat ihre erste Medaille* 1998 gewonnen und hat dann 2009 einen schweren Unfall gehabt. Im folgenden Jahr hat sie trotzdem ihr bestes Jahr gehabt und gewann bei den Winterspielen fünf Goldmedaillen.

Medaille (medal) has been explained, so you should be able to have a good guess at the compound noun *Goldmedaille* (Gold + Medaille – 'gold medal').

*Medaille – medal

Complete these sentences. Write the letter for the correct option in each box.

(a) Verena was blind …

A	from age 2.
B	from birth.
C	from age 18.

(1 mark)

(b) Verena's main interest was in …

A	winter sports.
B	athletics.
C	running.

(1 mark)

(c) She won her first medal in …

A	1998.
B	1989.
C	2009.

(1 mark)

(d) In 2009 she …

A	won five medals.
B	had an accident.
C	had her best year.

(1 mark)

Photo card

2 Talk about the content of these photos. You must say at least **one** thing about each photo.

(5 marks)

Photo 1

Photo 2

Listen to the recording

After you have spoken about the content of the photos, listen to the recording of further questions that relate to **any** of the topics within the theme of **Popular culture**. Pause the recording to give your answers. You should try to develop your answers as much as you can. **(20 marks)**

Celebrity culture Had a go ☐ Nearly there ☐ Nailed it! ☐

Celebrity events

Role play

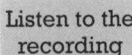
Listen to the recording

1. You are talking to your German friend.

   Listen to the recording of the teacher's part. The teacher will play the part of your friend and will speak first.

   You should address your friend as *du*.

   When you see this – **?** – you will have to ask a question.

   > 1 Say who your favourite celebrity is. (Give **two** details.)
   > 2 Give one negative aspect of being famous.
   > **?** 3 Ask your friend a question about a celebrity they like.
   > 4 Say whether you have been to a live concert.
   > 5 Say which band you would like to see in the future.

   > Note that some tasks specify the number of details you need to provide.

   (10 marks)

Translation

2. Translate the following sentences into **German**.

   My favourite star is a footballer.

   ....

   On Saturdays, I often go to the match.

   ....

   My brother always listens to music.

   ....

   We download videos from the internet.

   ....

   Last year, I saw a great concert in the park.

   ....

   (10 marks)

> Look first at the verb in each sentence. Note the person (*ich*, *er*, *wir*, etc) and the tense.

> The last sentence is in the past tense. You can use either the perfect or the imperfect tense to translate this.

> Consider word order rules – you need to think about inverting the verb and subject in the second and fifth sentences and about the separable verb in the fourth sentence.

Had a go ☐ Nearly there ☐ Nailed it! ☐   **Celebrity culture**

Celebrities for the environment

An environmental activist

1 You read this blog online.

> Ich habe normalerweise keine Zeit für Stars und solche Persönlichkeiten. Sie haben für mich sehr wenig zu bieten. Aber Greta Thunberg ist meiner Meinung nach ein echter Star, nicht weil sie schön oder reich ist und Designerkleidung trägt, sondern weil sie keine Angst hat, die Wahrheit zu sagen, für die Zukunft zu kämpfen und schwierige Fragen über die Umwelt zu stellen. Diese junge Frau hat solch einen positiven Einfluss auf junge Menschen in der ganzen Welt gehabt und hat auch die Meinungen der älteren Generation verändert. Ihre Initiative, einen Streik in den Schulen zu organisieren (*Fridays for Future* oder *Freitage für die Zukunft*), um Erwachsene zu überzeugen, dass sie mehr für den Klimaschutz tun sollen, war eine echte Inspiration. **Max**

Read the following statements and write the correct letters in each box.

Write **A** if only statement A is correct

  B if only statement B is correct

  A+B if both statements A and B are correct.

(a) **A** Max thinks that most celebrities are overpaid.

  B He has little interest in celebrity culture. ☐ **(1 mark)**

(b) **A** Max admires Greta Thunberg's courage.

  B He admires her fashion sense. ☐ **(1 mark)**

(c) **A** Max says Greta has had a real impact on young people worldwide.

  B He says she has made a difference to how adults think. ☐ **(1 mark)**

A caring celebrity

2 You read this article about a celebrity.

> Cate Blanchett ist nicht nur eine bekannte Schauspielerin, sie macht auch viel für die Umwelt. In einem Theater in Sydney, Australien, hat sie mit ihrem Mann eine Initiative für grüne Energie organisiert. Jetzt kommt der Strom direkt von der Sonne, denn das Gebäude hat 1900 Solarzellen*, die über 70% der Energie produzieren.
> Ihr nächster Plan war, wenn es regnet, das Wasser zu sammeln und zu benutzen. Das bedeutet, dass in der Zukunft das Theatergebäude klimaneutral** wird und die Umwelt gar nicht verschmutzt. Sie interessiert sich auch für Recycling und Wiederverwendung – man wirft also keine Kleidung weg, die man in einer Theaterproduktion benutzt hat. Alles kann für spätere Produktionen nützlich sein.

* *Solarzellen* – solar panels   ** *klimaneutral* – carbon neutral

Answer the following questions in **English**.

(a) What was the focus of Cate Blanchett's first environmental project?

....

(b) What did this project achieve? Give **two** details.

....

(c) How will the theatre become carbon neutral? Give **two** details.

....   **(5 marks)**

Travel and tourism

Had a go ☐ Nearly there ☐ Nailed it! ☐

Holiday activities

Holiday plans

1 Write a short post about an ideal holiday.

Write approximately **50** words in **German**.

You must write something about each bullet point.

Mention:
- the destination
- the journey
- the weather
- the activities
- the food.

> This is a short response question. You should aim to write about 10 words for each bullet point. Keep your sentences simple and stick with the present tense.

> Write a separate short paragraph for each point. Check that you have five sections in your response.

....
....
....
....
....
....
....
....
....
....
....

(10 marks)

Holidays

2 You hear a man talking about holidays.

Which destinations does he mention?

Complete the table in **English**.

Listen to the recording

when he was younger	now	in the future
(a) _____	(b) _____	(c) _____

(3 marks)

54

Had a go ☐ **Nearly there** ☐ **Nailed it!** ☐

Travel and tourism

Holiday accommodation

Dictation

1 Play the recording of four short sentences.

Listen carefully and using your knowledge of German sounds, write down in **German** exactly what you hear for each sentence.

You will hear each sentence **three** times: the first time as a full sentence, the second time in short sections and the third time again as a full sentence.

Use your knowledge of German sounds and grammar to make sure that what you have written makes sense. Check carefully that your spelling is accurate.

Sentence 1 ....

Sentence 2 ....

Sentence 3 ....

Sentence 4 .... **(8 marks)**

> Sounds to watch out for here:
> - ä – sounds like 'a' and 'e' combined
> - j – sounds like 'y'
> - sp – sound like 'shp'
> - final -e – as in *Tante*
> - ei – sounds like English 'I'
> - w – sounds like 'v'.
>
> Listen to the recording to practise these sounds.

Track 67

Reading aloud

2 Read aloud the following text in **German**.

> Wir fahren nicht jedes Jahr in Urlaub, weil es heute so teuer ist.
> Manchmal bleiben wir hier in der Gegend und machen mit dem Auto Tagesausflüge.
> Letzten Sommer waren wir in einem Ferienhaus an der Küste, was sehr schön war.
> Während der Woche haben wir in der Nähe ein Schloss besucht.

(5 marks)

> Sounds to watch out for here:
> - w – sounds like 'v' (*wir, weil*)
> - eu – sounds like 'oy' (*heute, teuer*)
> - ei – sounds like English 'I' (*bleiben, einem*)
> - final -d – sounds like 't' (*Gegend, und, während*)
> - ä – sounds like 'a' and 'e' combined (*Nähe*).
>
> Listen to the recording to practise these sounds.

Track 68

Now play the recording to listen to four questions in **German** related to the topic of **Travel and tourism**. In order to score the highest marks, you must try to **answer all four questions as fully as you can**. **(10 marks)**

> For the follow-on questions, develop your answers whenever possible.

Travel and tourism

Had a go ☐ Nearly there ☐ Nailed it! ☐

Other holiday accommodation

Reading aloud

1 Read aloud the following text in **German**.

> Ich fahre jedes Jahr in die Türkei.
> Dann kann ich meine Familie sehen.
> Ich wohne bei meiner Tante und meinem Onkel.
> Sie haben ein schönes Haus neben einem See.
> Meine Schwester und ich schlafen in einem Zelt.

(5 marks)

> Sounds to watch out for here:
> - long *a* – sounds like 'aah' in *fahre*
> - *-e* – at the end of the word is a separate syllable
> - *j* – sounds like 'y'
> - *ei* – sounds like English 'I'
> - *ö* – sounds like 'o' and 'e' combined
> - *ee* – not like the English 'ee' sound, but more like 'ay'
> - *sch* – sounds like 'sh'.
> Listen to the recording to practise these sounds.

Track 70

Listen to the recording

Now play the recording to listen to four questions in **German** related to the topic of **Travel and tourism**. In order to score the highest marks, you must try to **answer all four questions as fully as you can**.

(10 marks)

Reading aloud

2 Read aloud the following text in **German**.

> In den Ferien fahren wir oft nach Europa, wo das Wetter wärmer ist.
> Diesen Sommer bleiben wir aber in unserer Gegend und werden einige Tagesausflüge machen.
> Für mich ist das Wichtigste, Zeit mit Familie und Freunden zu verbringen.
> Wenn der Urlaub Spaß macht, ist es mir egal, wo das geschieht.

(5 marks)

> Sounds to watch out for here:
> - *eu* – sounds like 'oy'
> - *w* – sounds like 'v'
> - *ä* – sounds like 'a' and 'e' combined
> - *s* – a soft 's' sound, not a 'z' sound
> - *ei* – sounds like the English 'I'
> - *ü* – sounds like 'u' and 'e' combined – purse your lips to make this sound
> - *-e* – at the end of the word is a separate syllable
> - *z* – sounds like 'ts'
> - *ie* – sounds like the English 'ee'.
> Listen to the recording to practise these sounds.

Track 72

Listen to the recording

Now play the recording to listen to four questions in **German** related to the topic of **Travel and tourism**.

In order to score the highest marks, you must try to **answer all four questions as fully as you can**.

(10 marks)

Had a go ☐ Nearly there ☐ Nailed it! ☐

Travel and tourism

Opinions about travelling

Photo card

1 Talk about the content of these photos. You must say at least **one** thing about each photo. **(5 marks)**

Photo 1

Photo 2

> Say something about the people you see in the photo – male or female, age, clothes, appearance.

> Say where they are and what they are doing.

> Although the photo is in black and white, you can still use colour adjectives – this adds detail to your comments.

After you have spoken about the content of the photos, listen to the recording of further questions that relate to **any** of the topics within the theme of **Communication and the world around us**. Pause the recording to give your answers. You should try to develop your answers as much as you can.

(20 marks)

Types of transport

2 Write a blog post about types of transport.

Write approximately **50** words in **German**.

You must write something about each bullet point.

Mention:
- car driving
- cycling
- travel by bus
- travel by train
- flying.

> Remember to answer each bullet point in a separate short paragraph. You can aim to write about 10 words for each point, or you can write a longer response to a point where you have more to say.

....
....
....
....
....
....
....
....
....

(10 marks)

Travel and tourism

Had a go ☐   Nearly there ☐   Nailed it! ☐

Planning a future holiday

How I spend my summer holidays

1 You are writing a blog about summer holiday activities. Write approximately **90** words in **German**.

You must write something about each bullet point.

Describe:
- what you usually do in the summer holidays
- a place you have visited in the past
- what you are going to do this summer.

> You need to respond to **all three** bullet points.

> It's a good plan to write a paragraph for each point. If you have time at the end of the exam, you can go back and add another sentence if you have a new idea.

> Bear in mind that your paragraphs do not need to be of equal length, so develop those where you have most to say.

....
....
....
....
....
....
....
....
....
....

(15 marks)

Summer plans

2 Charlotte is telling you about her plans for the summer.

Which **three** of the following activities will she do this summer?

Write the correct letter in each box.

A	beach holiday
B	dancing
C	sport
D	seeing films
E	shopping
F	eating out

(a) ☐

(b) ☐

(c) ☐

> On the first listen, make a note of all the holiday activities you hear.

> Be careful to check **who** is going to do the activities – sometimes it may not be Charlotte!

(3 marks)

Had a go ☐ **Nearly there** ☐ **Nailed it!** ☐

Travel and tourism

Past holidays

Translation

1 Translate the following sentences into **German**.

The hotel was comfortable and modern.

....

There was a beautiful beach.

....

The people were very friendly.

....

I bought some presents for my friends and family.

....

The weather was good and it was warm every day.

.... **(10 marks)**

> Because this topic is about a past holiday, all the tasks here are in the past tense to give you some practice.

Translation

2 Translate the following sentences into **German**.

Last year, we went to Austria on holiday.

....

My grandparents live in the mountains there, so we do not need a hotel.

....

We stayed for a week and the weather was good the whole time.

....

I went swimming in the lake.

....

On the last day, we had a traditional lunch.

.... **(10 marks)**

> Usually, there will be only one past tense for you to tackle.

Travel and tourism

Had a go ☐ Nearly there ☐ Nailed it! ☐

Holiday problems

My holidays

1 You are writing to an Austrian friend about a past holiday.

Write approximately **90** words in **German**.

You must write something about each bullet point.

Describe:

- where you were on holiday
- what problems you had on holiday
- what you will do in the next holidays.

> You can use either the perfect tense (e.g. *ich bin … gefahren*) or the imperfect tense *(ich war, es gab)* to respond to the first two bullet points. The third bullet point is in the future, so use either a future tense (*ich werde … + infinitive*) or a future time phrase with a present tense (*Nächstes Jahr will ich … + infinitive / Nächstes Jahr fahre ich …*).

....
....
....
....
....
....
....
....
....

(15 marks)

Listen to the recording

Dictation

2 Play the recording of five short sentences.

Listen carefully and using your knowledge of German sounds, write down in **German** exactly what you hear for each sentence.

You will hear each sentence **three** times: the first time as a full sentence, the second time in short sections and the third time again as a full sentence.

Use your knowledge of German sounds and grammar to make sure that what you have written makes sense. Check carefully that your spelling is accurate.

Sentence 1 ....

Sentence 2 ....

Sentence 3 ....

Sentence 4 ....

Sentence 5 ....

(10 marks)

> Sounds to listen out for here:
> - *j* – sounds like 'y'
> - *w* – sounds like 'v'
> - *ö* – sounds like a combination of 'o' and 'e'
> - *ü* – sounds like a combination of 'u' and 'e', with pursed lips
> - *z* – sounds like 'ts'
> - *-e* – at the end of the word is a separate syllable.
>
> Listen to the recording to practise these sounds.

Track 77

Had a go ☐ Nearly there ☐ Nailed it! ☐

Travel and tourism

Making a complaint

Grammar task

1. Using your knowledge of grammar, complete the following sentences in **German**.

   Choose the correct German word from the three options in the grid.

   Write the correct **word** in the space, as shown in the example below.

   Example:

   Ich .....*gehe*..... heute in ein Café.

geht	gehe	gehen

   (a) Wir .... nur selten im Restaurant.

esst	esse	essen

   (b) Darf ich .... Karte sehen?

die	das	den

   (c) Ich habe den Fisch ....

bestellen	bestellt	bestellst

   (d) .... Vater trinkt Rotwein.

Mein	Meine	Meinen

   (e) Wir haben .... Hähnchen.

keine	keinen	kein

   > This short exercise is a test of essential basic German grammar. Think about:
   > - gender of nouns
   > - articles and cases
   > - adjective endings
   > - verb forms.

   (5 marks)

An evening at a restaurant

2. You are writing to a German friend about a night out in a restaurant.

   Write approximately **90** words in **German**.

   You must write something about each bullet point.

   Describe:
   - the occasion for your going out
   - what was wrong with the restaurant
   - whether you will eat at this restaurant in the future.

   > The third bullet point requires a future time frame, so you could use:
   > - *Ich werde …* + infinitive
   > - *In der Zukunft* + present tense
   > - *Ich will …* + infinitive
   > - *Ich möchte …* + infinitive.

   ....

   ....

   ....

   ....

   ....

   ....

   (15 marks)

Travel and tourism

Had a go ☐ Nearly there ☐ Nailed it! ☐

Lost property

Lost items

1. Four people are talking about lost items.

   What has each person lost?

   Write the correct letter in the box.

A	dog
B	handbag
C	jacket
D	money
E	phone
F	tickets

   (a) Emily ☐

   (b) Max ☐

   (c) Sascha ☐

   (d) Yusuf ☐

   (4 marks)

Translation

2. Translate the following sentences into **German**.

   On Tuesday last week, I travelled by train from Cologne to Munich.

   ....

   Unfortunately, because I was so tired, I fell asleep.

   ....

   I left my mobile phone on the train.

   ....

   The next morning, I went back to the station.

   ....

   I was lucky because someone found my phone and took it to the office.

   ....

   (10 marks)

> Due to the topic, all the sentences for translation are in the past tense, whereas in an exam, you will probably only have one past tense to deal with and most of the sentences will be in the present tense. This is a good opportunity for you to practise past tenses!

> Take particular care with verbs like *fahren*, *gehen* and *einschlafen* in the perfect tense. As they denote either movement from one place to another or a change of state, they use *sein* rather than *haben* to form their perfect tenses.

Had a go ☐ Nearly there ☐ Nailed it! ☐

Travel and tourism

Holiday jobs

Summer plans

1. Three friends are talking about their plans for the summer.

   What does each person plan to do?

   Write the correct letter in each box.

   > Use the first listen to get an initial idea of what each person says. You'll find it helpful to jot down some notes of what you hear.

   (a) What will Samira do this summer?

A	She plans to go away on holiday.
B	She plans to help her parents.
C	She plans to work in a shop.

   ☐

   > On the second listen, decide and write down your answers, checking them against your notes.

   (1 mark)

   (b) What does Layla plan to do?

A	She will move house.
B	She will play sport.
C	She will work one day a week.

   ☐ **(1 mark)**

   (c) What are Malik's plans?

A	He is going to stay with friends.
B	He is going to work on his English.
C	He is going to go away with his parents.

   ☐ **(1 mark)**

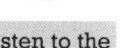

Last summer

2. Emily is talking about what she did last summer.

   Complete the sentences in **English**.

   Write **one** word in each space.

   Example:

   Before going to England, Emily felt ....nervous / worried........ .

   (a) She was in Cambridge for .... days. **(1 mark)**

   (b) She found staying with a family .... **(1 mark)**

   (c) Each day, she worked in a .... **(1 mark)**

   (d) She learned a lot of .... **(1 mark)**

   > Make some quick notes as you listen for the first time. If you note details in the right order, it will help you locate the information you need for your answers.

Travel and tourism

Had a go ☐   Nearly there ☐   Nailed it! ☐

Buying gifts and souvenirs

Buying gifts

Listen to the recording

1 You hear these conversations in a gift shop in Switzerland.

What do they want to buy and **for whom**?

Write the correct **letter** for the gift in the **What** box.

Write the correct **number** for the person in the **Who** box.

> Make quick notes of what you hear during the first listen.

> Listen closely to rule out what they decide **not** to buy.

What?

A	book
B	glass
C	T-shirt
D	water bottle

Who?

1	brother
2	mother
3	sister
4	stepbrother

	What?	Who?	
(a) Felix	☐	☐	(2 marks)
(a) Claudia	☐	☐	(2 marks)

Picture task

> Always start with the person or people in the picture – their appearance and their clothing.

> Move on to where they are and then what they are doing.

> You can make guesses, by saying *ich denke* or by using *vielleicht*.

2 You see this photo online.

What is in this photo?

Write **five** sentences in **German**.

....

....

....

....

....

(10 marks)

64

Had a go ☐ **Nearly there** ☐ **Nailed it!** ☐

Media and technology

Mobile technology

Why I find my phone essential

1 You read Yusuf's blog about mobile phones.

> Mein Handy ist für mich total nötig – aus vier Gründen. Grund eins – ohne Handy weiß ich nicht, was in der Welt passiert. Grund zwei – ohne das GPS-System kann ich meinen Weg durch die Stadt nicht finden. Grund drei – ohne Handy bekomme ich keine Nachrichten von Freunden und – Grund vier – ich kann keine lustigen Fotos sehen.

What are his reasons for saying his phone is vital?

Write the correct letter in each box.

A	hearing the news	D	playing online games
B	keeping in touch with friends	E	seeing amusing pictures
C	listening to music	F	not getting lost

> Read carefully through the text, making a quick note of the meaning of words you immediately recognise.

(a) Reason 1 ☐ (1 mark)

(b) Reason 2 ☐ (1 mark)

(c) Reason 3 ☐ (1 mark)

(d) Reason 4 ☐ (1 mark)

Dictation

2 Play the recording of five short sentences.

Listen carefully and using your knowledge of German sounds, write down in **German** exactly what you hear for each sentence.

You will hear each sentence **three** times: the first time as a full sentence, the second time in short sections and the third time again as a full sentence.

Use your knowledge of German sounds and grammar to make sure that what you have written makes sense. Check carefully that your spelling is accurate.

Sentence 1 ....

Sentence 2 ....

Sentence 3 ....

Sentence 4 ....

Sentence 5 .... **(10 marks)**

> Listen to this audio to practise these German sounds.
> - **g** – a hard sound, as at the start of the English word 'green'
> - **ie** – sounds like the English 'ee'
> - **ä** – sounds like a combined 'a' and 'e' sound (a bit like the 'a' in 'say')
> - **ch** – a soft throaty sound
> - **w** – sounds like 'v'
> - **ü** – sounds like 'u' and 'e' combined.
>
> Track 83

Media and technology

Had a go ☐ Nearly there ☐ Nailed it! ☐

Social media

How I use social media

1. You write to an Austrian friend about how you use technology and social media.

   Write approximately **50** words in **German**.

   You must write something about each bullet point. Mention:
   - your mobile
   - social networks
   - the internet
   - photos online
   - music.

   > Make sure that you respond to each bullet point. Practise writing about 10 words in response to each of them. You can write all your responses here in the present tense.

   ....
   ....
   ....
   ....
   ....
   ....

   (10 marks)

How I use social media

2. You are writing to a German friend about social media.

   Write approximately **90** words in **German**.

   You must write something about each bullet point.

   Describe:
   - the positive aspects of social media
   - how you have used social networks recently
   - how you will stay safe online in the future.

   > Answer all the bullet points in the correct tense – one requires the present, one the past and one the future. To aim high, try to develop and extend your ideas by adding further detail and make your opinions convincing by explaining them, using *denn* or *weil*.

   > Examples of more complex language structures will really enhance the quality of your work. Possible examples are *um … zu*, *wenn* clauses, *damit*, *wo* and modal verbs like *können*.

   ....
   ....
   ....
   ....
   ....
   ....
   ....
   ....
   ....

   > In the exam you will have more writing space, but here you can continue on your own paper if necessary.

   (15 marks)

Had a go ☐ **Nearly there** ☐ **Nailed it!** ☐

Media and technology

Internet

Target grades 5–9

Photo card

1 Talk about the content of these photos. You must say at least **one** thing about each photo.

(5 marks)

Photo 1

Photo 2

> You should refer to what the people are doing – using appropriate present tense verbs. For the first photo here, the verbs *lesen*, *arbeiten* and *lernen* will be useful, and for the second photo, you could use *sehen*, *ansehen* or *anschauen*.

Listen to the recording

After you have spoken about the content of the photos, listen to the recording of further questions that relate to **any** of the topics within the theme of **Communication and the world around us**. Pause the recording to give your answers. You should try to develop your answers as much as you can.

(20 marks)

Target grades 1–5

Translation

2 Translate these sentences into **English**.

Ich finde das Internet nötig.

....

Zu Hause haben wir einen neuen Computer.

....

Meine Eltern denken, ich verbringe zu viel Zeit online.

....

Gestern habe ich einen Film heruntergeladen.

....

Wenn ich Zeit habe, spiele ich gern Videospiele.

....

(10 marks)

Media and technology

Had a go ☐ Nearly there ☐ Nailed it! ☐

Computer games

Playing computer games

1 You are writing to a Swiss friend about computer games.

Write approximately **90** words in **German**.

You must write something about each bullet point.

Describe:
- whether you enjoy computer games
- which game(s) you have played recently
- a game you would like to try in the future.

> On a real Writing paper, this would be one of two options. Choose the option that you know most vocabulary and phrases for. You can invent your likes, dislikes and experiences – the important thing is that you aim to use the German you know correctly.

....
....
....
....
....
....
....
....
....
....
....
....
....
....

(15 marks)

Game preferences

2 You hear your German friend talking about computer games.

What sort of games does she mention?

Complete the table in **English**.

Listen to the recording

as a child	now	in the future
easy / fun games	(a)	(b) ....

(2 marks)

Had a go ☐ **Nearly there** ☐ **Nailed it!** ☐

Media and technology

Opinions about technology

Picture task

Write about the people you can see in the photo. How many are there? Are they male or female, young or older? What do they look like and what are they wearing?

You can begin your sentences with *Es gibt …* (There is/are …) or *Ich sehe …* (I can see …) or *Auf dem Foto gibt es …* (In the photo there is/are …).

If the photo is taken outside, as this one is, you could mention what the weather is like.

1 You see this photo on a social media site.

   What is in this photo?

   Write **five** sentences in **German**.

   ....
   ....
   ....
   ....
   .... **(10 marks)**

The benefits of technology

2 You are writing an article about technology.

   Write approximately **150** words in **German**.

   You must write something about both bullet points.

   Describe:
   - your opinions about the value of technology
   - how you think technology will improve your life in future.

   ....
   ....
   ....
   ....
   ....
   ....
   ....
   ....

You may continue your answer on your own paper if you do not have space here.

(25 marks)

Media and technology

Had a go ☐   Nearly there ☐   Nailed it! ☐

Films on the internet

Watching films

1 Mila is talking about streaming films.

What does she say?

Choose the correct answer and write the letter in each box.

(a) What is Mila's opinion of television?

A	She finds it boring.
B	She finds it interesting.
C	She finds it relaxing.

(b) What is the advantage of downloading films?

A	You have more choice.
B	You don't have to pay.
C	You can see the latest films.

(c) Where does Mila usually watch films?

A	In the living room.
B	In the dining room.
C	In the bedroom.

(d) Why might she pause the film?

A	To answer the phone.
B	To have a snack.
C	To walk her dog.

(4 marks)

> Make a note of some of the key words suggested by the options in the questions. So, for 'living room' you might note *Wohnzimmer*, and for 'snack' *etwas essen*. Then check whether you hear these words in the recording.

Translation

2 Translate these sentences into **English**.

Im einundzwanzigsten Jahrhundert brauchen wir kein traditionelles Fernsehen mehr.

....

Das ist nun eine sehr alte Technologie.

....

Heute haben wir das Internet und die Möglichkeit, alle Arten von Sendungen anzuschauen.

....

Mit Netflix kann man sehen, was man will, und auch die Uhrzeit wählen.

....

Gestern habe ich mir einen interessanten Film über Arbeitsplätze für junge Leute angesehen.

....

(10 marks)

> Make notes as you read through the text for the first time, to capture the words you know. Then try to translate a chunk of language at a time – stop at commas and full stops as they mark a natural break. If there are words you don't know, try to work them out and have a go, rather than leaving a gap.

Had a go ☐ Nearly there ☐ Nailed it! ☐

The environment and where people live

My home

Target grades 1–5

Translation

1 Translate the following sentences into **German**.

   My house is quite modern.

   ....

   There is a large kitchen.

   ....

   I like my bedroom because it is comfortable.

   ....

   In the evening, we often watch a film.

   ....

   Last weekend, he worked in the garden.

   .... **(10 marks)**

> Watch out for dative case here – remember that it is used to describe the position / location of something so after prepositions like *in*.

Target grades 5–9

Dictation

2 Play the recording of five short sentences.

   Listen carefully and using your knowledge of German sounds, write down in **German** exactly what you hear for each sentence.

   You will hear each sentence **three** times: the first time as a full sentence, the second time in short sections and the third time again as a full sentence.

   Use your knowledge of German sounds and grammar to make sure that what you have written makes sense. Check carefully that your spelling is accurate.

   Sentence 1 ....

   Sentence 2 ....

   Sentence 3 ....

   Sentence 4 ....

   Sentence 5 .... **(10 marks)**

> Sounds to watch out for here:
> - *w* – sounds like 'v'
> - *st* – sounds like 'sht'
> - long *a* – as in *mag*
> - *ei* – sounds like the English 'I'
> - final *-ig* – also sounds like *ich*
> - long *o* – sounds like 'oh'
> - *ch* – throaty sound, as in *ich*
> - *z* – sounds like 'ts'
> - *qu* – sounds like 'kv'.
>
> Listen to the recording to practise these sounds.
>
> Track 88

The environment and where people live

Had a go ☐ Nearly there ☐ Nailed it! ☐

My town

Picture task

> Remember to mention the people, place and activity.

> The weather would be a good thing to mention here too.

> Remember that you can start your sentences with *Es gibt …* (There is / are …) or *Ich sehe …* (I can see …).

1 You see this photo on social media.

   What is in this photo?

   Write **five** sentences in **German**.

   ....
   ....
   ....
   ....
   .... **(10 marks)**

Target grades 7–8

Where I live

Listen to the recording

2 Your friend Felix is talking about his town.

   What does he say about it?

   Write **A** if only statement **A** is correct

        B if only statement **B** is correct

        A+B if both statements **A** and **B** are correct.

   (a) Felix says the town …

A	is a cultural centre.
B	has a lot of industry.

   (b) He says that …

A	there are seven famous bridges.
B	there is a riverside market every weekend.

   > Check the time references – how often does the market take place?

   (c) He says the town has …

A	a successful music centre.
B	a very modern art gallery.

   > Check which adjective describes which noun! Is it the music centre which is historic or the art gallery?

   (3 marks)

Had a go ☐   Nearly there ☐   Nailed it! ☐   **The environment and where people live**

Facilities in town

Photo card

1 Talk about the content of these photos. You must say at least **one** thing about each photo.

(5 marks)

Photo 1   **Photo 2**

After you have spoken about the content of the photos, listen to the recording of further questions that relate to **any** of the topics within the theme of **Communication and the world around us**. Pause the recording to give your answers. You should try to develop your answers as much as you can.

(20 marks)

> There's a lot to say here. Some suggestions for Photo 1:
> - It's outside in a street, the people are on foot and it looks like summer.
> - There are lots of people – describe what one or two are wearing.
> - People are walking, chatting, shopping and carrying bags.
>
> And for Photo 2:
> - There are four young people, two girls and two boys.
> - They are shopping.
> - The girls are carrying bags.

Grammar task

2 Using your knowledge of grammar, complete the following sentences in **German**.

Choose the correct German word from the three options in the grid.

Write the correct **word** in the space, as shown in the example below.

Example:

Ich ......*gehe*........ in die Stadt.

geht	gehe	gehen

(a) .... du am Samstag einkaufen gehen?

Will	Willst	Wollen

(b) Es gibt ein .... Kino in der Stadt.

moderner	moderne	modernes

(c) Mein Bruder .... oft Kleidung.

kauft	kaufe	kaufen

(d) Wir kaufen Gemüse auf .... Markt.

der	dem	das

(e) .... bin jetzt im Café.

Er	Wir	Ich

> The idea of this exercise is to test your understanding of basic grammar. The focus is on:
> - nouns and genders
> - adjective endings
> - articles in different cases
> - verb forms / verb and subject agreement.

(5 marks)

The environment and where people live

Had a go ☐ Nearly there ☐ Nailed it! ☐

Finding the way

Target grades 3–4

Which way?

1 You hear these people asking for and receiving directions.

What is each person looking for and which way should they go?

Write the correct **letter** for the place.

Write the correct **number** for the way.

	Place
A	beach
B	bus station
C	church
D	post office

	Which way?
1	left
2	left then right
3	right
4	straight along the street

- Try to think of the destinations in the first grid in German (*Strand*, etc), then each of the directions (*links*, etc).
- Make quick notes in the correct order during the first listen and write down some answers if you can.
- Check your notes and answer the questions during the second listen.

	Place	Which way?	
(a) Anton	☐	☐	(2 marks)
(b) Nadia	☐	☐	(2 marks)
(c) Steffi	☐	☐	(2 marks)

Target grades 7–8

Asking for directions

2 You hear this conversation in the street. Choose the correct answer and write the letter in each box.

(a) Where does the man want to go?

A	To the cinema.
B	To the hotel.
C	To the station.

☐

(b) What should he do first?

A	Stay on this street.
B	Turn left.
C	Turn right.

☐

(c) What will he then come to?

A	A bridge.
B	A library.
C	A park.

☐

(d) What should he do after turning left?

A	Take the second street on the left.
B	Take the second street on the right.
C	Take the third street on the right.

☐

(e) What should he then do?

A	Turn left at the café.
B	Turn left at the cinema.
C	Turn left at the stadium.

☐

(f) What is at the other side of the marketplace?

A	The bus station.
B	The train station.
C	The underground station.

☐

(6 marks)

Had a go ☐ Nearly there ☐ Nailed it! ☐

The environment and where people live

Shops and shopping

Picture task

> Say something about the person you can see in the picture – gender, mood and clothes can all be mentioned.

> Say something about the location of the picture, e.g. 'He is in a shop.'

> Finally, say what the person is doing, e.g. 'He is shopping.' or 'He is buying new clothes.'

1 You see this photo on Instagram.

What is in this photo?

Write **five** sentences in **German**.

....

....

....

....

.... **(10 marks)**

Photo card

2 Talk about the content of these photos. You must say at least **one** thing about each photo.

(5 marks)

Photo 1   **Photo 2**

> Put together *Buch* and *Laden* to make *Buchladen* (m) to describe the location in the first photo.

After you have spoken about the content of the photos, listen to the recording of further questions that relate to **any** of the topics within the theme of **Communication and the world around us**. Pause the recording to give your answers. You should try to develop your answers as much as you can.

(20 marks)

> Express some opinions / ideas and explain them if possible by using *ich denke, ich finde, meiner Meinung nach …* and then *denn* or *weil*.

The environment and where people live

Had a go ☐ Nearly there ☐ Nailed it! ☐

Shopping in town

At the market

1 You hear four German teenagers shopping at the market.

   What does each person want to buy?

   Write the correct letter in the box.

A	a bag	D	coffee
B	a book	E	clothes
C	cake	F	vegetables

> Before the recording starts, look at the options and think what each one could be in German. This will help you to focus on what you hear and to notice which items are not mentioned.

(a) Jonas ☐ **(1 mark)**

(b) Mia ☐ **(1 mark)**

(c) Jamal ☐ **(1 mark)**

(d) Amina ☐ **(1 mark)**

Dictation

2 Play the recording of five short sentences.

Listen carefully and using your knowledge of German sounds, write down in **German** exactly what you hear for each sentence.

You will hear each sentence **three** times: the first time as a full sentence, the second time in short sections and the third time again as a full sentence.

Use your knowledge of German sounds and grammar to make sure that what you have written makes sense. Check carefully that your spelling is accurate.

Sentence 1 ....

Sentence 2 ....

Sentence 3 ....

Sentence 4 ....

Sentence 5 ....

(10 marks)

> Listen out for key German sound symbol correspondences and remember the German pronunciation rules you know. Don't forget that two of the words will be from outside the vocabulary list, and for these words the rules mentioned are even more important.

> Some key sounds here are:
> - ä – sounds like a combined 'a' and 'e' sound (a bit like 'ay' in 'say')
> - v – sounds like 'f'
> - äu – sounds like 'oy'
> - ö – sounds like 'o' and 'e' combined
> - w – sounds like 'v'
> - final -e – as in *Handtasche*
> - au – sounds like 'ow'.
>
> Listen to the recording to practise these sounds.

Had a go ☐ Nearly there ☐ Nailed it! ☐   **The environment and where people live**

Transport

Getting around

1 You are writing to a German friend about transport.

Write approximately **90** words in **German**.

You must write something about each bullet point.

Describe:

- transport where you live
- a recent trip
- how you will get to your next holiday destination.

> Check the tense of the task before you start writing. It's a good idea to note down on the exam paper which task is in which tense.

> There will always be **three** different time frames in this type of question (past, present and future, including the conditional form), which appears on both the Higher and Foundation tier papers.

....
....
....
....
....
....
....
....
....
.... **(15 marks)**

Translation

2 Translate these sentences into **English**.

Die öffentlichen Verkehrsmittel in meiner Gegend sind wirklich schrecklich.

....

Der Grund dafür ist, dass ich in einem Dorf auf dem Land wohne.

....

Es gibt wenige Busse, und wir müssen deshalb das Auto benutzen.

....

Gestern hat mein Bruder mich zur Schule gefahren.

....

Es regnete stark, und ich konnte nicht mit dem Fahrrad fahren.

.... **(10 marks)**

> Check through your finished translation to make sure it sounds like usual English. If it doesn't, you may need to think about rephrasing. An example here is *es regnete stark*, which literally means 'it was raining strongly'. Ask yourself how you would express this idea – you could write 'it was raining hard / heavily' or 'it was pouring down / with rain'.

The environment and where people live

Had a go ☐   Nearly there ☐   Nailed it! ☐

Travelling by train

At the ticket office

1 You hear this conversation at the train station.

Choose the correct answer. Write the letter in each box.

Listen to the recording

(a) The young woman wants to go to …

A	Munich.
B	Berlin.
C	Cologne.

(b) She wants to leave …

A	this evening.
B	this afternoon.
C	tomorrow morning.

(c) She will arrive at her destination at …

A	8 am.
B	8 pm.
C	11 pm.

(d) Her ticket costs …

A	93 euros.
B	30 euros.
C	39 euros.

(4 marks)

> Remember that for travel purposes the 24-hour clock is used; so, for example, *19:00 Uhr* is 7 pm.

Asking about train times

2 You hear this conversation at the train station.

Write **A** if only statement **A** is correct

B if only statement **B** is correct

A+B if both statements **A and B** are correct.

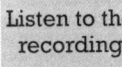

Listen to the recording

(a) The woman …

| A | wants to travel today. |
| B | wants to go to Munich. |

(b) There is a train at …

| A | 12 noon. |
| B | 1 pm. |

(c) There is also …

| A | a train at 3:30 pm. |
| B | a later train at 6 pm. |

(d) She will …

| A | arrive at 8 pm. |
| B | have to reserve a seat. |

(4 marks)

> Times are mentioned here referring to train departures and arrivals. This is a key element of the question, so focus on these times and make a note of them as you listen.

> Remember that the 24-hour clock is used in the world of travel, so 12 noon is *zwölf Uhr*, but 1 pm is *dreizehn / 13 Uhr*! So what would 3:30 pm and 6 pm be?

Had a go ☐ **Nearly there** ☐ **Nailed it!** ☐

The environment and where people live

The environment and me

Role play

1 You are talking to your German friend.

Listen to the recording of the teacher's part. The teacher will play the part of your friend and will speak first.

You should address your friend as *du*.

When you see this – **?** – you will have to ask a question.

> 1 Say something about the environment where you live. (Give **two** details.)
>
> ?2 Ask your German friend a question about environmental problems.
>
> 3 Say why the environment important to you. (Give **two** details.)
>
> 4 Say what you have done recently to help the environment. (Give **two** details.)
>
> 5 Say what you will do in future to protect the environment.

Remember: In order to score full marks, you must include at least one verb in your response to each task.

Dictation

2 Play the recording of four short sentences.

Listen carefully and using your knowledge of German sounds, write down in **German** exactly what you hear for each sentence.

You will hear each sentence **three** times: the first time as a full sentence, the second time in short sections and the third time again as a full sentence.

Use your knowledge of German sounds and grammar to make sure that what you have written makes sense. Check carefully that your spelling is accurate.

Sentence 1

....

Sentence 2

....

Sentence 3

....

Sentence 4

....

(8 marks)

> Sounds to listen out for here:
> - *st* – sounds like 'sht'
> - *au* – sounds like 'ow'
> - *ä* – sounds like 'a' and 'e' combined
> - *o* – a long sound in some words, e.g. *groß*
> - *e* – a long sound in some words, e.g. *Problem*
> - *a* – a short sound in some words, e.g. *Abfall*
> - *w* – sounds like 'v'.
>
> Listen to the recording to practise these sounds.
>
> Track 101

The environment and where people live

Had a go ☐ Nearly there ☐ Nailed it! ☐

Environmental problems

Reading aloud

1   Read aloud the following text in **German**.

> Es gibt heute viele Umweltprobleme.
> Die Temperaturen steigen immer weiter.
> Die Meere sind schmutzig, und Fische und Vögel sterben.
> Wir sollten unsere Erde besser schützen.
> In der Zukunft wird es vielleicht nicht genug Wasser geben.

(5 marks)

> Sounds to watch out for here:
> - v – sounds like a soft 'f'
> - w – sounds like 'v'
> - -e – remember that an -e at the end is pronounced as a separate syllable
> - ö – sounds like a combination of 'o' and 'e'
> - ü – sounds like a combination of 'u' and 'e'
> - z – sounds like 'ts'
> - -d – a final -d sounds like 't'.
>
> Listen to the recording to practise these sounds.
>
> Track 102

Listen to the recording

Now play the recording to listen to four questions in **German** related to the topic of **The environment and where people live**.

In order to score the highest marks, you must try to **answer all four questions as fully as you can**.

(10 marks)

Photo card

2   Talk about the content of this photo.   **(5 marks)**

> This is an unusual photo to describe.
> - It has two parts which are very different, so perhaps try to say something about the right-hand side and then the left-hand side.
> - For the purposes of this exercise, you only have one photo to describe. But remember that in the exam there will be two, both of which you need to mention in your description.
> - You could use *auf der rechten Seite* and *auf der linken Seite* …
> - There is also a person for you to say something about – a man, walking across a field, wearing trousers and a T-shirt.
> - Feel free to include colour adjectives in your description, even though the photo here is black and white. This will be good practice for the exam photos.

Listen to the recording

After you have spoken about the content of the photo, listen to the recording of further questions that relate to **any** of the topics within the theme of **Communication and the world around us**. Pause the recording to give your answers. You should try to develop your answers as much as you can.

(20 marks)

Had a go ☐   Nearly there ☐   Nailed it! ☐   The environment and where people live

The dangers of pollution

Dictation

1 Play the recording of four short sentences.

Listen to the recording

Listen carefully and using your knowledge of German sounds, write down in **German** exactly what you hear for each sentence.

You will hear each sentence **three** times: the first time as a full sentence, the second time in short sections and the third time again as a full sentence.

Use your knowledge of German sounds and grammar to make sure that what you have written makes sense. Check carefully that your spelling is accurate.

Sentence 1 ....

Sentence 2 ....

Sentence 3 ....

Sentence 4 ....   **(8 marks)**

> Sounds to listen out for here:
> - ö – sounds like 'o' and 'e' combined
> - sp – sounds like 'shp'
> - -e – final -e is a sounded syllable
> - w – sounds like 'v'
> - sch – sounds like 'sh'.
>
> Listen to the recording to practise these sounds.
>
> Track 106

Photo card

2 Talk about the content of these photos. You must say at least **one** thing about each photo.

(5 marks)

Photo 1

Photo 2

> Start with the people – their appearance, clothing and mood. Then say something about the place – as it's an outdoor shot, you could mention the weather. Then describe what they are doing. Don't panic if you don't know some vocabulary – instead find things you *can* say. They are collecting / finding / looking for paper / rubbish. They are making the park clean. They are helping the environment. They are putting bottles in a bag.

> Remember: even though the image is in black and white, you can still comment on the colours you think things might be. For example, that they are wearing green T-shirts.

The environment and where people live

Had a go ☐ Nearly there ☐ Nailed it! ☐

Individual actions for the environment

Protecting the environment

1. You are writing to a Swiss friend about the environment.

   Write approximately **90** words in **German**.

   You must write something about each bullet point.

   Describe:
   - what you do to protect the environment
   - what you have recycled recently
   - how you will live an environmentally-friendly life in future.

   > Make sure you write something in response to each bullet point. It's OK to write more for one than for another, just don't miss one out.

   > Remember that the second bullet point on this question is always in the **past** tense and the third in the **future** tense, so use verb forms which reflect this.

   ....
   ....
   ....
   ....
   ....
   ....
   ....
   ....
   ....
   ....

   (15 marks)

Reading aloud

2. Read aloud the following text in **German**.

   > Ich habe große Angst um unsere Umwelt.
   > Ich denke, wir haben die Welt mit Verschmutzung kaputt gemacht.
   > Das schlimmste Problem heute ist der Klimawandel.
   > Wir sehen jetzt oft Wetterveränderungen, und die Welt wird wärmer.
   > Wir brauchen bessere Gesetze, um die Erde und das Meer zu schützen, und ich hoffe, dass es nicht zu spät ist.

   (5 marks)

   > Sounds to watch out for here:
   > - w – sounds like 'v'
   > - j – sounds like 'y'
   > - z – sounds like 'ts'
   > - ü – sounds like a combination of 'u' and 'e'
   > - ä – sounds like a combination of 'a' and 'e'.
   >
   > Listen to the recording to practise these sounds.

   Track 107

Listen to the recording

Now play the recording to listen to four questions in **German** related to the topic of **The environment and where people live**.

In order to score the highest marks, you must try to **answer all four questions as fully as you can**.

(10 marks)

Had a go ☐ Nearly there ☐ Nailed it! ☐   **The environment and where people live**

How to recycle

Picture task

> Mention the people in the photo first – their age, clothing and appearance.
>
> Mention where they are – here, outside, in the garden, at home.
>
> You can begin your sentences with *Es gibt* … or *Ich sehe* … This gives you a strong starting point for each response.

1 You see this photo online.

What is in this photo?

Write **five** sentences in **German.**

....
....
....
....
.... **(10 marks)**

Translation

2 Translate the following sentences into **German**.

> Remember: you need a reflexive verb to say 'I am interested in'.

I am interested in the environment and want to protect it.

....

So I always separate the rubbish at home and throw paper in the blue sack*.

....

It is not difficult and everyone should do it.

....

If you do this, you can recycle many things.

....

Yesterday, I worked with a group to clean the park.

.... **(10 marks)**

*sack – *Sack* (m)

> How would you say 'so'? You can use *deshalb* which means 'because of this' or 'that's why'.

> Remember the rule about modal verbs like *sollen* sending the infinitive to the end of the sentence.

The environment and where people live

Had a go ☐ Nearly there ☐ Nailed it! ☐

Weather

Picture task

> As they are outside, this is an opportunity to describe the weather.

> Use colour adjectives to develop your answers where appropriate, even though the photo is in black and white.

1 You see this photo on Instagram.

What is in this photo?

Write **five** sentences in **German.**

....

....

....

....

.... **(10 marks)**

Weather report

2 You read a weather report on driving conditions in Switzerland.

> **Straßenwetter**
>
> In der Nacht auf Donnerstag wird es nicht lange regnen. Trotzdem wird es später sehr kalt mit Minusgraden, und in höheren Lagen sind die Straßen mit Schnee bedeckt*. Bei Fahrten in die Höhe brauchen Sie Winterreifen** für Ihr Auto. Einige Straßen in den Bergen sind geschlossen. Das MeteoNews-Team wünscht Ihnen eine gute und sichere Fahrt.

* *bedeckt* – covered

** *Winterreifen* – winter tyres

Complete the sentences in **English**. Write **one** word in each space.

(a) On Thursday night, there will not be much .... **(1 mark)**

(b) It will be .... later. **(1 mark)**

(c) There will be .... on higher roads. **(1 mark)**

(d) Some mountain roads are .... **(1 mark)**

> Read the text first to get a rough idea of the content.
>
> Then look at the questions and refer back to the text to spot where the answers are located.

> Remember that the questions follow the order of the information given in the text.

Had a go ☐   Nearly there ☐   Nailed it! ☐

The environment and where people live

The natural world

Translation

1 Translate these sentences into **English**.

Ich wohne in einem Dorf auf dem Land.

....

Die frische Luft ist gesund.

....

In meiner Gegend gibt es viele Bäume.

....

Letztes Wochenende sind wir in dem Wald wandern gegangen.

....

Es gefällt mir, hier zu leben.

....   **(10 marks)**

> Check the main verb and its subject in each sentence. Check which tense the verb is in – one will not be in the present tense.
>
> Now look at the nouns and other elements to see how they fit with the verbs.
>
> Then look at which words are left. If you're not sure what they mean, make an intelligent guess instead of leaving a gap.

> Take care with the final sentence where *gefallen* is used. Remember that this means 'to please' and is used to say what someone likes.

Listen to the recording

Where I live

2 You listen to Paul describing the area where he lives.

Complete the sentences in **English**.

Write **one** word in each space.

(a) Paul's home town is between the .... and the mountains.   **(1 mark)**

(b) Paul is glad that there is no ....   **(1 mark)**

(c) A popular attraction for tourists is the summer ....   **(1 mark)**

(d) Outside the town there are .... paths.   **(1 mark)**

(e) The river is .... for swimming.   **(1 mark)**

> Remember that the questions reflect the order in which the information appears in the recording.

> There will also be distractors – words that are mentioned but which are not the required answer – so you need to listen closely for more specific detail: *(nicht viel) Verschmutzung* is an example here.

About the exams

Had a go ☐ Nearly there ☐ Nailed it! ☐

Practice for Paper 1: Listening

Practise for the Listening tasks with this selection of exam-style questions.

Target grades 2–3

Track 110

Free-time activities

1 Jana and Malik are talking about activities with friends.

What do they say?

Write the correct letter in each box.

Answer all parts of question 1.

1.1 What will Jana and her friend do first?

A	Go to the café.
B	Go to the book shop.
C	Go to the library.

1.2 What will they do next?

A	Go to the café.
B	Go shopping.
C	Go for a walk.

1.3 What will Malik and his friend do?

A	Buy a computer.
B	Buy a game.
C	Buy a football.

1.4 What does Jana say she prefers?

A	She prefers dancing.
B	She prefers fashion.
C	She prefers music.

(4 marks)

Target grades 1–5

Track 111

Dictation

2 Play the recording of four short sentences.

Listen carefully and using your knowledge of German sounds, write down in **German** exactly what you hear for each sentence.

You will hear each sentence **three** times: the first time as a full sentence, the second time in short sections and the third time again as a full sentence.

Use your knowledge of German sounds and grammar to make sure that what you have written makes sense. Check carefully that your spelling is accurate.

Sentence 1

....

Sentence 2

....

Sentence 3

....

Sentence 4

....

(8 marks)

Remember that two of the words you will hear are not from the vocabulary list, so it is important for you to listen particularly closely to these and think about how to write down the sounds you hear.

Had a go ☐ Nearly there ☐ Nailed it! ☐

About the exams

Practice for Paper 1: Listening

Practise for the Listening tasks with this selection of exam-style questions.

Target grades 5–6

Track 112

Working life

1 You hear Lara and Arda talking about their jobs.

What do they like and dislike about their jobs?

Write the correct letter in each box.

A	boss	D	pay
B	co-workers	E	projects
C	hours of work	F	workspace

                  Likes   **Dislikes**

1 Lara   ☐   ☐   **(2 marks)**

2 Arda   ☐   ☐   **(2 marks)**

Target grades 5–9

Track 113

Dictation

2 Play the recording of five short sentences.

Listen carefully and using your knowledge of German sounds, write down in **German** exactly what you hear for each sentence.

You will hear each sentence **three** times: the first time as a full sentence, the second time in short sections and the third time again as a full sentence.

Use your knowledge of German sounds and grammar to make sure that what you have written makes sense. Check carefully that your spelling is accurate.

Sentence 1

....

....

Sentence 2

....

....

Sentence 3

....

....

Sentence 4

....

....

Sentence 5

....

.... **(10 marks)**

About the exams

Had a go ☐ Nearly there ☐ Nailed it! ☐

Practice for Paper 2: Speaking

Practise for the Speaking tasks with this selection of exam-style questions.

Target grades 1–5

Role play

Track 114

1 You are talking to your German friend.

Listen to the recording of the teacher's part. The teacher will play the part of your friend and will speak first.

You should address your friend as *du*.

When you see this – **?** – you will have to ask a question.

> **In order to score full marks, you must include a verb in your response to each task.**
> 1 Say what you do in your free time.
> 2 Say what you think of music.
> ?3 Ask your friend a question about their free time.
> 4 Say how often you go to the cinema.
> 5 Say what your plans are for this weekend.

(10 marks)

Target grades 1–5

Reading aloud

2 Read aloud the following text in **German**.

> Meine Stadt ist sauber.
> Ich mag die frische Luft.
> Wir haben viele schöne Parks in der Gegend.
> Ich fahre jeden Tag mit dem Fahrrad zur Schule.
> Das ist besser für die Umwelt als ein Auto.

Track 115

(5 marks)

Now play the recording of four questions which relate to the topic of **Free-time activities**.

In order to score the highest marks, you must try to **answer all four questions as fully as you can**.

(10 marks)

Target grades 1–5

Photo card

3 Look at the two photos as part of your preparation. Make as many notes as you want on an Additional Answer Sheet for use during the test.

Track 116

You will be asked about the content of these photos by your teacher. The recommended time is approximately **one minute. You must say at least one thing about each photo.** **(5 marks)**

After you have spoken about the content of the photos, play the recording to hear some questions related to **any** of the topics within the theme of **People and lifestyle**. **(20 marks)**

Photo 1

Photo 2

Had a go ☐ Nearly there ☐ Nailed it! ☐

About the exams

Practice for Paper 2: Speaking

Practise for the Speaking tasks with this selection of exam-style questions.

Role play

1. You are talking to your Swiss friend.

   Listen to the recording of the teacher's part. The teacher will play the part of your friend and will speak first.

   You should address your friend as *du*.

   When you see this – **?** – you will have to ask a question.

   > **In order to score full marks, you must include at least one verb in your response to each task.**
   > 1 Say how often you play sport.
   > 2 Say why you think sport is important. (Give **two** details.)
   > 3 Say what you think of computer games. (Give **one** opinion and **one** reason.)
   > 4 Say what you will eat and drink this evening.
   > ?5 Ask your friend a question about their lifestyle.

   (10 marks)

Reading aloud

2. Read aloud the following text in **German**.

   > Ich versuche, jeden Tag Sport zu treiben.
   > Das hilft mir, gesund und aktiv zu bleiben.
   > Meine Lieblingssportart ist Tennis, denn man kann bei gutem Wetter draußen spielen.
   > Ich bin Mitglied in einem Verein, der regelmäßig gegen andere Clubs in der Region spielt.
   > Jeden August in den Sommerferien nehmen wir an einem nationalen Wettbewerb teil.

   (5 marks)

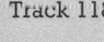

   Now play the recording of four questions which relate to the topic of **Free-time activities**.

   In order to score the highest marks, you must try to **answer all four questions as fully as you can.**

   (10 marks)

Photo card

3. Look at the two photos as part of your preparation. Make as many notes as you want on an Additional Answer Sheet for use during the test.

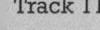

   You will be asked about the content of these photos by your teacher. The recommended time is approximately **one minute. You must say at least one thing about each photo.** **(5 marks)**

   After you have spoken about the content of the photos, you will then be asked questions related to **any** of the topics within the theme of **Communication and the world around us**. **(20 marks)**

Photo 1

Photo 2

About the exams

Had a go ☐   Nearly there ☐   Nailed it! ☐

Practice for Paper 3: Reading

Practise for the Reading tasks with this selection of exam-style questions.

Life in a town

1 You read Noah's blog about his town.

> Meine Stadt war früher eine Industriestadt und hatte vor zwanzig Jahren viele Fabriken*. Jetzt gibt es keine Industrie mehr, und die Stadt ist ruhiger und sauberer als sie damals war.
>
> Die Stadt ist heute das kulturelle Zentrum der Region, und es gibt ein interessantes Museum und Kunstgalerien, und auch ein sehr aktives Nachtleben, mit vielen Clubs und Bars, wo man einen lustigen Abend verbringen kann.
>
> Der Sonntagsmarkt neben dem Fluss ist auch sehr beliebt, und viele Touristen besuchen ihn, um Essen oder lokale Produkte zu kaufen. Es gibt zum Beispiel guten Käse und tolle **Lederwaren** wie Handtaschen und Schuhe.

* *Fabriken* – factories

Complete these sentences. Write the letter for the correct option in each box.

1 Noah's town used to be …

A	dirtier.
B	cleaner.
C	quieter.

(1 mark)

2 The town is now known for its …

A	culture.
B	music scene.
C	restaurants.

(1 mark)

3 The market takes place …

A	at Christmas.
B	once a week.
C	twice a week.

(1 mark)

4 Read the last sentence again. What does **Lederwaren** mean?

A	food items
B	plants
C	leather goods

(1 mark)

Translation

2 Translate these sentences into **English**.

Ich bin gesund.

……………………………………………………………………………………… (2 marks)

Ich esse jeden Tag Obst und Gemüse.

……………………………………………………………………………………… (2 marks)

Einmal in der Woche gehe ich ins Fitnesszentrum.

……………………………………………………………………………………… (2 marks)

Gestern habe ich eine Tanzstunde gehabt.

……………………………………………………………………………………… (2 marks)

Ich bin glücklicher, wenn ich mich bewege.

……………………………………………………………………………………… (2 marks)

Had a go ☐   Nearly there ☐   Nailed it! ☐   **About the exams**

Practice for Paper 3: Reading

Practise for the Reading tasks with this selection of exam-style questions.

Environmental issues

1 You read Sascha's blog about the environment.

> Unsere Welt leidet. Die Wälder werden zerstört und viele Tierarten verschwinden. Das ist klar, wenn man sich die Zeit nimmt, die Nachrichten zu hören oder eine Zeitung zu lesen. Viele Leute wollen diese schlimme Wahrheit aber nicht sehen, und machen so weiter, als ob alles in Ordnung wäre.
>
> Ich finde diese Denkweise gar nicht intelligent. Deshalb bin ich Mitglied einer Umweltorganisation, die versucht, etwas Positives gegen Umweltverschmutzung und Klimawandel zu tun. Wir haben keine Zeit zu verlieren, und müssen sofort hier und heute etwas machen. Die Lage ist jetzt echt ernst. Die einzige Lösung ist, dass wir unsere Lebensweise sofort verändern.

Answer the following questions in **English**.

1 What does Sascha say about the world?

.... **(1 mark)**

2 What examples does he give of environmental damage? Give **two** details.

....

.... **(2 marks)**

3 What attitude does Sascha find unintelligent?

.... **(1 mark)**

4 What does Sascha see as the only solution?

.... **(1 mark)**

Translation

2 Translate these sentences into **English**.

Wenn die Schule vorbei ist, möchte ich auf die Uni gehen, um ein Studium zu machen.

....

....

Mein Lieblingsfach ist Geschichte, denn ich interessiere mich für die Ereignisse der Vergangenheit.

....

....

Ich freue mich darauf, meine Stadt zu verlassen.

....

Das Leben hier kann etwas langweilig sein, und ich brauche neue Erfahrungen.

....

Ich hoffe, viele neue Leute kennenzulernen.

.... **(10 marks)**

About the exams

Had a go ☐ Nearly there ☐ Nailed it! ☐

Practice for Paper 4: Writing

Practise for the Writing tasks with this selection of exam-style questions.

My home town

1 A German friend is coming to stay.

Write a short description of your home town.

Write approximately **50** words in **German**.

You must write something about each bullet point.

Mention:
- the town
- the facilities in town
- the environment
- the transport
- the local area.

> Remember to write something for each bullet.
>
> Write about 10 words for each bullet.
>
> Check that any adjectives have the correct agreements.

....
....
....
....
.... **(10 marks)**

My school

2 You are writing to a German friend about your school.

Write approximately **90** words in **German**.

You must write something about each bullet point.

Describe:
- what your school is like
- something you have done at school recently
- what you would like to do next year.

> Remember to write something for each bullet.
>
> Make sure you use the correct time frame – the second bullet point requires a past tense and the third bullet point needs a future tense.

....
....
....
....
....
....
....
.... **(15 marks)**

Had a go ☐ Nearly there ☐ Nailed it! ☐

About the exams

Practice for Paper 4: Writing

Practise for the Writing tasks with this selection of exam-style questions.

Target grades 4–6

Healthy living

1 You are writing to a German friend about healthy living.

Write approximately **90** words in **German**.

You must write something about each bullet point.

Describe:

- what you do to keep fit
- what you did last week to be healthy
- what you will do in the future to keep fit.

....
....
....
....
....
....
....

(15 marks)

Target grades 5–9

Technology

2 Write a blog about technology in your life.

Write approximately **150** words in **German**.

You must write something about both bullet points.

Describe:

- how you make use of technology
- how you think technology will improve life in the future.

....
....
....
....
....
....
....
....
....
....

(25 marks)

93

Grammar

Had a go ☐ **Nearly there** ☐ **Nailed it!** ☐

Gender and plurals

> German nouns are **masculine** (m), **feminine** (f) or **neuter** (nt).
>
> With the **definite** article (the) they look like this:
>
> **der** Mann / **der** Tisch   **die** Frau / **die** Tür   **das** Kind / **das** Buch

1 Circle the correct definite article.

(a) der / die / **(das)** Mädchen (nt)
(b) **der** / die / das Lehrer (m)
(c) der / **die** / das Karte (f)
(d) der / die / **das** Flugzeug (nt)
(e) der / die / **das** Klassenzimmer (nt)
(f) der / **die** / das Schule (f)
(g) **der** / die / das Stuhl (m)
(h) der / **die** / das Tante (f)

2 Complete each sentence with *der*, *die* or *das*.

(a) .... Die .... Lehrerin ist freundlich. (f)
(b) .... Zimmer ist bequem. (nt)
(c) .... Handy ist toll. (nt)
(d) .... Zug fährt schnell. (m)
(e) .... Bahnhof ist nicht weit von hier. (m)
(f) .... Umwelt ist wichtig. (f)

> **Plurals** in German are formed in several different ways.
>
> Some add *-e* or *-n / -en*, others add an umlaut or an umlaut plus another letter, and some don't change.
>
> - (sg) Tisch –> (pl) Tisch**e**
> - (sg) Karte –> (pl) Karte**n**
> - (sg) Sohn –> (pl) S**ö**hn**e**
> - (sg) Mann –> (pl) M**ä**nn**er**
> - (sg) Freundin –> (pl) Freundin**nen**
> - (sg) Mädchen –> (pl) Mädchen

3 Are these nouns singular (sg), plural (pl) or could they be either singular or plural (sg / pl)?

(a) Frauen   .... pl ....
(b) Welt   ....
(c) Kinder   ....
(d) Lehrer   ....
(e) Bücher   ....
(f) Geld   ....
(g) Arbeit   ....
(h) Hausaufgaben   ....
(i) Schwimmbad   ....
(j) Mädchen   ....

Had a go ☐ Nearly there ☐ Nailed it! ☐   **Grammar**

Indefinite articles and possessives

> German nouns are **masculine** (m), **feminine** (f) or **neuter** (nt).
> With the **indefinite** article (a / an) they look like this:
> **ein** Mann / **ein** Tisch   **eine** Frau / **eine** Schule   **ein** Kind / **ein** Buch

1 Circle the correct indefinite article.
   (a) **(ein)** / **eine** Haus (*nt*)
   (b) **ein** / **eine** Lehrerin (*f*)
   (c) **ein** / **eine** Zug (*m*)
   (d) **ein** / **eine** Hotel (*nt*)
   (e) **ein** / **eine** Familie (*f*)
   (f) **ein** / **eine** Zimmer (*nt*)
   (g) **ein** / **eine** Stadt (*f*)
   (h) **ein** / **eine** Stück (*nt*)
   (i) **ein** / **eine** Kuchen (*m*)
   (j) **ein** / **eine** Junge (*m*)

> *kein / keine / kein* (not a / no) follows the same pattern as *ein / eine / ein*.
> The plural of *kein* is *keine*.
> **kein** Mensch (*m*)   **keine** Idee (*f*)   **kein** Haus (*nt*)   **keine** Hausaufgaben (*pl*)

2 Write the correct form of *kein / keine / kein*.
   (a) ......*kein*...... Buch (*nt*)
   (b) .... Bruder (*m*)
   (c) .... Schwestern (*pl*)
   (d) .... Brot (*nt*)
   (e) .... Lehrerin (*f*)

> The **possessives** follow the same pattern as *ein* and *kein*.
> **mein** Haus (*nt*)   **unser** Auto (*nt*)
> **dein** Bruder (*m*)   **eure** Freunde (*pl*)
> **seine** Schwester (*f*)   **Ihre** Arbeit (*f*)
> **ihre** Freundin (*f*)   **ihre** Interessen (*pl*)

3 Write these phrases in **German**.
   (a) *my sister*   *meine Schwester*   (f) *my homework*   ....
   (b) *your family* (*du* form) .... (g) *his jacket*   ....
   (c) *his wife*   ....   (h) *her party*   ....
   (d) *her boyfriend*   ....   (i) *your clothes*   ....
   (e) *our town*   ....   (j) *my glass*   ....

Grammar — Had a go ☐ Nearly there ☐ Nailed it! ☐

Nominative and accusative cases

The **nominative** case is used for the **subject** of the sentence.

With *der / die / das*:

Der Mann wartet auf den Bus. **Die** Frau ist jung. **Das** Kind ist klein. **Die** Bücher sind schwer.

With *ein, kein* or a possessive:

Mein Bruder ist groß. **Keine** Lehrerin ist da. **Unser** Haus ist klein. Wo sind **meine** Schuhe?

The **accusative** case is used for the **direct object** of the sentence. The word for 'the / a' changes in the **masculine accusative**. There is no change in the other genders or the plural.

With *der / die / das*:

	m	f	nt	pl
nominative	der	die	das	die
accusative	**den**	die	das	die

Siehst du **den** Mann?

With *eine / kein* and possessives:

	m	f	nt	pl
nominative	ein	eine	ein	keine
accusative	**einen**	eine	ein	keine

Hast du **einen** Bruder?

---

1 Complete the sentences with the correct missing form of *der / die / das*. Remember to check whether you need the nominative or accusative!

  (a) ......*Der*...... Lehrer kommt spät.

  (b) .... Mädchen sieht .... Film.

  (c) .... Junge hat .... Buch.

  (d) .... Frau kauft .... Zeitung.

  (e) .... Kinder haben .... Ball verloren.

  (f) .... Touristen besuchen .... Museum.

  (g) .... Mann hat .... Karten gekauft.

  (h) .... Jugendlichen kaufen .... Computerspiel.

2 Complete the sentences with the correct missing form of *ein / eine / ein*. Remember to check whether you need the nominative or accusative!

  (a) Hat sie ......*einen*...... Bruder oder .... Schwester?

  (b) Wir haben .... großes Frühstück gegessen.

  (c) Hast du .... Garten zu Hause?

  (d) Ich habe .... Film gesehen.

  (e) Haben Sie .... Stadtplan?

  (f) Gibt es hier .... Restaurant?

3 Circle the correct possessives needed to complete each sentence.

  (a) **Mein /** (**Meine**) **/ Mein** Schwester hat **meinen / meine / mein** Rock.

  (b) Ist **dein / deine / dein** Freund hier?

  (c) **Mein / Meine / Mein** Onkel liest **seinen / seine / sein** Zeitung.

  (d) **Ihr / Ihre / Ihr** Mann arbeitet im Ausland.

  (e) Das ist **unser / unsere / unser** Problem.

  (f) **Mein / Meine / Mein** Noten sind nicht so gut.

Had a go ☐ Nearly there ☐ Nailed it! ☐   **Grammar**

Other cases and prepositions

In addition to the nominative (used for the subject of the sentence) and the accusative (used for the direct object and after some prepositions), you also need to know how to use the **dative** and **genitive** cases. Here is a reminder of what happens to articles in these cases.

Definite articles (*der / die / das*) and *dieser / jeder / welcher*:

	m	f	nt	pl
dative	dem	der	dem	den
genitive	des	der	des	der

Indefinite articles (*eine / kein*) and possessives:

	m	f	nt	pl
dative	einem	einer	einem	keinen
genitive	eines	einer	eines	keiner

Note that the endings are the same with both the definite and indefinite articles, so you only need to learn them once.

1 Underline the dative article and noun in each sentence.

   (a) Ich gebe <u>der</u> <u>Lehrerin</u> meine Hausaufgaben.
   (b) Wir laufen aus dem Haus.
   (c) Er kauft seiner Mutter ein Buch.
   (d) Ich habe meinem Vater im Garten geholfen.
   (e) Sie geht mit ihren Freunden aus.
   (f) Ich erzähle meinen Eltern alles.

> Note that when you use a noun in the dative plural, you add an -*n* to the end of the noun if it does not already end in -*n*.

2 Some set phrases use the dative case. What do these ones mean?

   (a) im Ausland ....
   (b) an der Küste ....
   (c) auf dem Land ....
   (d) bei uns ....
   (e) im Gegenteil ....

3 Complete each sentence with the correct form of *der / die / das* in the genitive case. You may sometimes need to add an -*s* to the noun.

   (a) Der Bruder .... des .... Mädchen .... s .... ist ziemlich sportlich.
   (b) In der Mitte .... Stadt ist ein Markt.
   (c) Trotz .... Wetter .... gehen wir zelten.
   (d) Während .... Sommerferien spiele ich Basketball.
   (e) Die Arbeit .... Ärzte ist sehr hart.

4 Translate the sentences from Exercise 3 into **English**.

   (a) ....
   (b) ....
   (c) ....
   (d) ....
   (e) ....

Grammar

Had a go ☐ Nearly there ☐ Nailed it! ☐

Prepositions with the accusative or dative

The **dual case** prepositions are:

an *on (vertically), at*
auf *on (horizontally)*
in *in*
hinter *behind*
neben *next to*
über *over / above*
unter *under / below*
vor *in front of / before*
zwischen *between*

- Use the **accusative** case to express *movement towards* a different location, e.g. going into the house.
- Use the **dative** when there is a fixed position and *no movement* to a different location, e.g. remaining in the house.

1 Circle the correct article to complete each sentence.

(a) Gehst du heute in **die** / **der** Stadt?

(b) Der Hund schläft in **den** / **dem** Garten.

(c) Wir schwimmen in **das** / **dem** Meer.

(d) Die Bücher sind auf **den** / **dem** Tisch.

(e) Die Bilder sind an **die** / **der** Wand.

(f) Sie gehen schnell in **das** / **dem** Haus.

(g) Wir wohnen neben (**dem**)/ **der** Fluss.

(h) Die Geschenke sind unter **den** / **dem** Baum.

(i) Die Katze läuft unter **das** / **dem** Bett.

(j) Es gibt einen Parkplatz hinter **den** / **dem** Fitness-Studio.

(k) Ich setze mich vor **den** / **dem** Computer.

(l) Das Café ist zwischen **den** / **dem** Kino und **die** / **der** Schule.

Some verbs are used with a preposition followed by the **accusative** case.

2 Complete the sentences with an accusative definite article (the).

(a) Meine Schwester und ich sprechen über .... Problem.

(b) Ich warte auf .... nächsten Zug.

(c) Die Schüler denken an .... Zukunft.

3 Now translate the sentences from Exercise 2 into **English**.

(a) ....

(b) ....

(c) ....

98

Had a go ☐ Nearly there ☐ Nailed it! ☐   **Grammar**

Dieser, jeder and *welcher*

Dieser, *jeder* and *welcher* all follow the *der / die / das* pattern.

	masculine	feminine	neuter	plural
nominative	dieser	diese	dieses	diese
accusative	diesen	diese	dieses	diese
dative	diesem	dieser	diesem	diesen
genitive	dieses	dieser	dieses	dieser

1 Add the correct ending to each word. Check whether you need to use the nominative, accusative or dative case.

(a) Dies ......e...... Stadt ist klein. (*f*)

(b) In jed .... Stadt gibt es ein Kino. (*f*)

(c) Ich mag dies .... Film. (*m*)

(d) Ich besuche dies .... Schule. (*f*)

(e) Welch .... Kinder spielen ein Instrument? (*pl*)

(f) Dies .... Junge wohnt in der Nähe. (*m*)

(g) Ich habe dies .... Buch schon gelesen. (*nt*)

(h) Welch .... Fluss ist der längste in der Schweiz. (*m*)

(i) Mit dies .... Bus kann man zum Stadion fahren. (*m*)

(j) Er geht mit dies .... Mädchen aus. (*nt*)

2 Complete the sentences with the correct word endings.

(a) Welch ......en...... Mann hast du gesehen?

(b) Mit welch .... Zug fahren Sie?

(c) Ich wohne in dies .... Hotel.

(d) Dies .... Woche bin ich in München.

(e) Am Ende dies .... Jahres werde ich ein Auto kaufen.

(f) Warum hast du dies .... Buch mit?

(g) Jed .... Schülerin muss eine Uniform tragen.

(h) Jed .... Mensch braucht eine Pause.

(i) Jed .... Stunde dauert 40 Minuten.

(j) In jed .... Klassenzimmer gibt es Laptops.

(k) Jed .... Flugzeug kommt heute spät an.

(l) Es gibt ein Geschenk für jed .... Kind.

Dieser and *jeder* are often used in **time expressions**.
In this context, they are used in the **accusative** case.
Jeden Monat – *every month*   **Diesen** Freitag – *this Friday*

3 Complete each word to give a time expression in the accusative case.

(a) jed ......es...... Jahr

(b) dies .... Woche

(c) dies .... Monat

(d) jed .... Wochenende

(e) jed .... Sonntag

Adjective endings

Had a go ☐ Nearly there ☐ Nailed it! ☐

Adjectives after definite articles

	masculine	feminine	neuter	plural
nominative	der alte Mann	die alte Frau	das alte Haus	die alten Häuser
accusative	den alten Mann	die alte Frau	das alte Haus	die alten Häuser
dative	dem alten Mann	der alten Frau	dem alten Haus	den alten Häusern
genitive	des alten Mannes	der alten Frau	des alten Hauses	der alten Häuser

1 Complete the sentences with the correct adjective endings. Check the gender, case and number (whether the noun is singular or plural).

(a) Die schwarz ....e........ Hose gefällt mir am besten. (*f*)

(b) Hast du den neu .... Lehrer gesehen? (*m*)

(c) Ich habe die weiß .... Schuhe gekauft. (*pl*)

(d) Ich liebe den braun .... Hund. (*m*)

(e) Wo ist das bekannt .... Museum? (*nt*)

Adjectives after indefinite articles

	masculine	feminine	neuter	plural
nominative	ein alter Mann	eine alte Frau	ein altes Haus	keine alten Häuser
accusative	einen alten Mann	eine alte Frau	ein altes Haus	keine alten Häuser
dative	einem alten Mann	einer alten Frau	einem alten Haus	keinen alten Häusern
genitive	eines alten Mannes	einer alten Frau	eines alten Hauses	keiner alten Häuser

2 Complete the sentences with the correct adjective endings. Check the gender, case and number.

(a) Mein klein ....er........ Bruder ist sehr sportlich. (*m*)

(b) Hast du eine älter .... Schwester? (*f*)

(c) Ich habe gestern ein interessant .... Buch gekauft. (*nt*)

(d) Wir versuchen, ein gesund .... Leben zu haben. (*nt*)

(e) Die Familie sucht eine klein .... Wohnung in der Nähe. (*f*)

(f) Seine best .... Freunde feiern seinen Geburtstag. (*pl*)

Adjectives without an article

	masculine	feminine	neuter	plural
nominative	schwarzer Kaffee	kalte Milch	gutes Wetter	nette Leute
accusative	schwarzen Kaffee	kalte Milch	gutes Wetter	nette Leute
dative	schwarzem Kaffee	kalter Milch	gutem Wetter	netten Leuten
genitive	schwarzen Kaffees	kalter Milch	guten Wetters	netter Leute

3 Complete the sentences with the correct adjective endings. Check the gender, case and number.

(a) Trinkst du gern schwarz ....en........ Kaffee? (*m*)

(b) Frisch .... Wasser schmeckt gut. (*nt*)

(c) Wir haben freundlich .... Lehrer. (*pl*)

(d) Ich esse am liebsten weiß .... Käse. (*m*)

Had a go ☐   Nearly there ☐   Nailed it! ☐   **Grammar**

Comparative and superlative adjectives and adverbs

Comparing adjectives and adverbs
Describing nouns:

adjective	comparative form + *-er*	superlative form + *-(e)st*
schnell	schneller	schnellst-
lustig	lustiger	lustigst-
interessant	interessanter	interessant**e**st-

Describing verbs:

adverb	comparative form + *-er*	superlative form *am ...* + *-(e)sten*
schnell	schneller	am schnellsten
lustig	lustiger	am lustigsten
interessant	interessanter	am interessant**e**sten

1. Complete the sentences with the correct comparative form of the adjective in brackets.

    (a) Ich finde Deutsch ......*interessanter*...... als Mathe. (*interessant*)

    (b) Mein Bruder ist .... als ich. (*intelligent*)

    (c) Es ist .... , mit dem Fahrrad zu fahren, als zu Fuß zu gehen. (*schnell*)

    (d) Ist deine Schwester .... als du? (*klein*)

 2. Complete the sentences with the correct superlative form of the adjective in brackets.

    (a) Dies ist das ....*modernste*........ Haus auf der Straße. (*modern*)

    (b) Ich finde Physik das .... Fach. (*schwer*)

    (c) Cricket ist das .... Spiel. (*langsam*)

    (d) Diese Hose ist die .... im Geschäft. (*teuer*)

 3. Complete the sentences with the correct comparative and superlative forms of the adverb in **bold**.

    (a) Lea singt **schön**, aber Matteo singt ....*schöner*.......... und Anna singt ....

    (b) Max läuft **schnell**. Yuki läuft .... als Max, aber ich laufe ....

> Some comparative / superlative forms are **irregular**. Many common single-syllable adjectives add an umlaut too: *wärmer / kälter / länger*. And some are even more irregular: *gut / besser / best-*, *gern / lieber / liebst-* and *hoch / höher / höchst-*.

4. Translate these sentences **into English**.

    (a) Mein Vater ist größer als ich. ....

    (b) Wie heißt der höchste Berg in der Schweiz? ....

    (c) Was für Filme siehst du am liebsten? ....

Personal pronouns

Here's a reminder of how the personal pronouns work in the three main cases.

nominative	accusative	dative
ich	mich	mir
du	dich	dir
er / sie / es	ihn / sie / es	ihm / ihr / ihm
wir	uns	uns
ihr	euch	euch
Sie	Sie	Ihnen
sie	sie	ihnen

Plural dative forms are only needed at Higher tier.

1 Complete the sentences with the correct pronoun in the appropriate case.

(a) Was machst ....du............ heute Abend? (*you, familiar sg*)

(b) Kommt ihr mit .... ? (*us*)

(c) Meine Mutter ist lieb. Ich verstehe mich gut mit .... (*her*)

(d) Kannst du .... helfen? (*me*)

(e) Ich zeige .... den Weg. (*you, formal*)

(f) Ich rufe .... später an. (*you, familiar sg*)

(g) Er hat .... nicht gekannt. (*her*)

(h) Ich schicke .... eine Geburtstagskarte. (*him*)

(i) Hast du .... heute gesehen? (*them*)

(j) Warte! Ich komme mit .... (*you, familiar sg*)

> Some set phrases are always used with a **dative** pronoun.
> Es geht mir gut. *I'm fine.*
> Wie geht es dir? *How are you?*
> Das schmeckt mir. *It tastes good / I like the taste.*
> Mir ist kalt / warm! *I'm cold / hot.*
> Es gelingt uns, ... zu + infinitive. *We manage to ...*
> Es tut mir leid. *I'm sorry.*
> Es ist mir egal. *I'm not bothered.*
> ... gefällt mir. *I like ...*

2 Complete the sentences with the correct pronoun in the dative case.

(a) Wie geht es ....euch............ ? (*you, familiar pl*)

(b) Es tut .... leid. (*we / us*)

(c) Das ist .... egal. (*I / me*)

(d) Der Film gefällt .... (*he / him*)

(e) Wie schmeckt es .... ? (*you, familiar sg*)

(f) Es ist .... gelungen, den Berg zu steigen. (*she / her*)

Had a go ☐ Nearly there ☐ Nailed it! ☐ **Grammar**

Word order 1

> The first rule of German word order is that **the verb is the second 'idea'** (chunk of language) in a sentence. If something else is added at the front, the verb inverts (the subject and verb swap places).
>
> Ich **fahre** nach Köln. –> Morgen **fahre** ich nach Köln.

1 Rewrite these sentences after adding the phrase in brackets at the front.

Example: Ich gehe zu Fuß zur Schule. (*Jeden Tag*) –> Jeden Tag **gehe** ich zu Fuß zur Schule.

(a) Wir fahren in die Schweiz. (*Nächstes Jahr*)

....

(b) Mein Bruder geht im Park laufen. (*Jeden Morgen*)

....

(c) Ich lerne sehr gerne Englisch. (*In der Schule*)

....

(d) Meine Freunde spielen Fußball. (*In den Ferien*)

....

> **Word order in the perfect tense**
>
> The key rule is that the past participle stands at the end of the clause / sentence. The part of *haben* or *sein* is the main verb and is the second idea. Inversion rules still apply.

2 Rewrite these jumbled sentences in the correct order. Start with the word / phrase in **bold**.

(a) gehabt / mein Freund / hat / **Letzte Woche** / eine Party

....

(b) aus dem Fenster / ist / gesprungen / die Katze / **Plötzlich**

....

(c) sind / wegen des Wetters / angekommen / spät / **Wir** / in Berlin

....

> **Word order in the future tense and with modal verbs**
>
> With these structures, the infinitive stands at the end of the clause or sentence, while the part of *werden* (for the future tense) or the modal verb (e.g. *ich will, wir konnten, ich musste, man darf*, etc) is the main verb and is the second idea. Inversion rules still apply.

3 Rewrite these present tense sentences in the future tense.

(a) Er spielt morgen Golf. ....

(b) Wann gehst du einkaufen? ....

(c) Nächstes Jahr verlasse ich die Schule. ....

4 Rewrite these sentences to include the modal verb in brackets.

(a) Ich mache zuerst meine Hausaufgaben. (*müssen*) ....

(b) Meine Schwester fährt nach London. (*wollen*) ....

(c) Bald haben wir endlich mehr Freizeit. (*können*) ....

103

Grammar

Had a go ☐ **Nearly there** ☐ **Nailed it!** ☐

Conjunctions

A really useful and important **subordinating conjunction** is *weil* (because). By using this word, you can not only explain ideas and opinions, but you can also use some complex language, as *weil* moves the verb to the end of the clause or sentence.

Ich mag Mathe, **weil** ich einen tollen Lehrer **habe**.

1 Link these pairs of sentences together using *weil*.

> Remember to use a comma before *weil* and move the verb to the end.

Example: Ich bin heute müde. Ich habe zu viele Hausaufgaben. –>
Ich bin heute müde, **weil** ich zu viele Hausaufgabe **habe**.

(a) Wir bleiben diesen Sommer zu Hause. Reisen ist sehr teuer.

....

(b) Ich will in der Zukunft studieren. Ich will Arzt werden.

....

(c) Er geht auf dem Land wandern. Das Wetter ist schön.

....

(d) Mein Bruder geht zu jedem Fußballspiel. Er ist ein großer Fan.

....

(e) Wir sollen die Umwelt besser schützen. Es gibt nur eine Welt.

....

Other conjunctions which work exactly like *weil* are: *als, bevor, bis, da, damit, dass, nachdem, ob, obwohl, während, was, wie* and *wenn*.

2 Rewrite these sentences, adding the conjunction shown in brackets in the position indicated.

> Check your punctuation and word order!

(a) Es war sehr spät. (*als*) Ich bin nach Hause gekommen.

....

(b) (*bevor*) Er geht zur Arbeit. Er isst das Frühstück.

....

(c) Die Lehrerin hilft uns. (*damit*) Wir verstehen besser.

....

(d) Wir wollten ausgehen. (*da*) Ich hatte Geburtstag.

....

(e) Die Studenten wissen. (*dass*) Sie müssen hart arbeiten.

....

3 Translate the sentences in Exercise 2 into **English**.

(a) ....
(b) ....
(c) ....
(d) ....
(e) ....

Had a go ☐ Nearly there ☐ Nailed it! ☐   **Grammar**

Word order 2

An **um ... zu + infinitive** (in order to ...) clause is a great way to develop an initial idea and use complex language. All you need to remember is to put a comma before *um* and put *zu* and the infinitive at the end.

Ich gehe ins Einkaufszentrum, **um** ein Geschenk für meinen Freund **zu kaufen**.

 1 Link these pairs of sentences and rephrase them using *um ... zu*.

Example: Ich gehe jeden Tag schwimmen. Ich bleibe fit. –>
Ich gehe jeden Tag schwimmen, **um** fit **zu** bleiben.

(a) Wir fahren dieses Jahr in den Urlaub. Wir genießen die Sonne.

....

(b) Ich werde nach London fahren. Ich suche eine Arbeitsstelle.

....

(c) Er fährt auf dem Land Fahrrad. Er ist an der frischen Luft.

....

Similarly, you can use **zu + infinitive** clauses after certain verbs. This is another great way of expressing yourself in more extended sentences.

Try these: *hoffen ... zu, versuchen ... zu, beginnen ... zu*.

 2 Rewrite these sentences to include the verb shown in brackets.

Example: Ich verdiene genug Geld. (*versuchen*) –>
Ich **versuche**, genug Geld **zu verdienen**.

(a) Ich mache nächstes Jahr ein Auslandsjahr*. (*hoffen*)

....

(b) Wir leben gesünder. (*versuchen*)

....

(c) Mein Freund treibt mehr Sport. (*beginnen*)

....

* *ein Auslandsjahr* – a year abroad

Relative clauses can also be used to develop and extend an initial idea. These clauses are introduced by the correct form of *der / die / das*, etc (meaning 'who / whom / which / that'), depending on the person or thing they refer to and its case. The relative clause is divided from the main clause by commas and the verb goes at the end of the clause.

Die Prüfungen, **die** wir dieses Jahr machen, beginnen im Mai.

3 Complete each sentence by selecting the correct relative pronoun from the three options provided. Consider both the gender and number of the noun it refers to and the case required within the relative clause.

(a) Der Mann, **(der)** / **den** / **das** da steht, ist der neue Mathelehrer.

(b) Das Mädchen, **das** / **die** / **der** rote Haare hat, heißt Hanna.

(c) Kennst du die Frau, **der** / **das** / **die** neben dir wohnt?

(d) Der Film, **den** / **der** / **dem** wir gestern Abend gesehen haben, war eine Komödie.

(e) Die Bücher, **das** / **die** / **den** wir lesen, sind nicht so spannend.

Grammar

Had a go ☐ Nearly there ☐ Nailed it! ☐

The present tense

Regular verbs in the present tense
Remove the *-en* ending to find the stem, then add these endings according to the person doing the action of the verb.

ich	spiel**e**	*I play / am playing*
du	spiel**st**	*you play / are playing*
er / sie / es	spiel**t**	*he / she / it plays / is playing*
wir	spiel**en**	*we play / are playing*
ihr	spiel**t**	*you play / are playing*
Sie	spiel**en**	*you play / are playing*
sie	spiel**en**	*they play / are playing*

1 Complete each sentence with the correct form of the verb in brackets. All these verbs are regular in the present tense.

  (a) Ich .... *wohne* .... in Köln. (*wohnen*)

  (b) Wir .... Basketball. (*spielen*)

  (c) Wie oft .... du schwimmen? (*gehen*)

  (d) Er .... oft Computerspiele. (*kaufen*)

  (e) Warum .... Sie? (*lachen*)

  (f) Was .... ihr heute Abend? (*machen*)

  (g) Mein Bruder .... das Abendessen. (*kochen*)

  (h) .... du ihn? (*lieben*)

  (i) Die Freunde .... sich E-Mails. (*schicken*)

  (j) .... du heute das Schloss? (*besuchen*)

  (k) Die Klasse .... hart. (*arbeiten*)

  (l) Wann .... die Sendung? (*beginnen*)

Some common verbs have a vowel change in the *du* and the *er / sie / es* forms.
For example, *fahren* –> *er fährt*   *geben* –> *er gibt*   *sehen* –> *er sieht*
You can check for vowel changes in the second column of the irregular verb tables on pages 108 and 109 of the Revision Guide. The endings are regular.

2 Complete each sentence with the correct form of the verb in brackets.

  (a) Wann .... *fährst* .... du nach Österreich? (*fahren*)

  (b) Ich .... am Montagabend. (*fahren*)

  (c) Wir .... einen Roman. (*lesen*)

  (d) Was .... du? (*lesen*)

  (e) Lena .... sehr gut Englisch. (*sprechen*)

  (f) Was .... er dir zum Geburtstag? (*geben*)

  (g) Mein Bruder .... immer noch. (*schlafen*)

  (h) Er .... uns später. (*treffen*)

  (i) Meine Freundin .... schöne Kleidung. (*tragen*)

  (j) Das Kind .... seiner Mutter. (*helfen*)

Had a go ☐ Nearly there ☐ Nailed it! ☐   **Grammar**

Reflexive and separable verbs

1. Match these reflexive verbs to their English meanings.

(a)	sich anziehen	(i)	to meet
(b)	sich bewegen	(ii)	to decide
(c)	sich treffen	(iii)	to get dressed
(d)	sich entscheiden	(iv)	to wonder
(e)	sich fragen	(v)	to apologise / excuse yourself
(f)	sich entschuldigen	(vi)	to move / take exercise

2. Complete each sentence with the correct reflexive pronoun.

   (a) Wir freuen .... auf das Wochenende.

   (b) Ich bewege .... nicht oft genug.

   (c) Er soll .... entschuldigen.

   (d) Sie zieht .... schnell an.

   (e) Wir treffen .... in dem Park.

   (f) Ich entscheide .... sofort.

3. Complete each sentence in the **present** tense with the two correct parts of the separable verb in brackets.

   Example: Wir ...*stehen*... zu spät ...*auf*... . (aufstehen)

   (a) Er .... immer früh .... (ankommen)

   (b) Ich .... meine Mutter .... (anrufen)

   (c) Meine Eltern .... bald .... (zurückkommen)

   (d) Heute Abend .... ich einen Film .... (herunterladen)

   (e) Mein Freund und ich .... samstags .... (ausgehen)

4. Complete these sentences in the **perfect** tense with the correct past participle of the verb in brackets.

   Example: Er ist am Nachmittag ...*ausgegangen*... . (ausgehen)

   (a) Ich bin heute Morgen .... (zurückkommen)

   (b) Der Lehrer hat meine Eltern .... (anrufen)

   (c) Ich habe lustige Fotos .... (hochladen)

   (d) Meine Tante ist gestern bei uns .... (ankommen)

   (e) Wir haben zusammen .... (fernsehen)

5. Rewrite these sentences in the correct order. All use separable verbs in the **future** tense. Start with the words in **bold**.

   (a) ankommen / in der Schweiz / morgen / **Ich** / werde

   (b) **Später** / Musikvideos / wird / im Internet / er / ansehen

   (c) früh / aufstehen / **Meine Eltern** / werden / morgen

Grammar — Had a go ☐ Nearly there ☐ Nailed it! ☐

Irregular verb tables 1

Refer to the irregular verb tables on page 108 of the Revision Guide to check the verb forms you need to use here.

> **Irregular verbs in the present tense**
>
> Look at the second column of the verb table to see which, if any, changes happen to the *er / sie / es* form of the verb. Any change will apply to the *du* form too.

1 Circle the correct form of the verb to complete each sentence.

   (a) Was **esse** / **(isst)** / **esst** du zu Mittag?

   (b) Er **fährst** / **fährt** / **fahrt** mit dem Zug.

   (c) Es **gibt** / **gebe** / **gebt** zu viele Leute.

   (d) Was **habe** / **habt** / **hast** du in der Tasche?

   (e) Die Lehrerin **helft** / **hilft** / **helfe** uns mit der Aufgabe.

   (f) Wie oft **lauft** / **läufst** / **läuft** du?

> **Irregular verbs in the imperfect tense**
>
> Use the third column of the verb tables to find the imperfect tense *er / sie / es* form. This is also the *ich* form and it acts as the stem to which appropriate endings are added for the other parts of the verb, e.g. *-st* for the *du* form and *-en* for the *wir / Sie / sie* forms.

2 Complete each sentence with the correct imperfect form of the verb in brackets.

   Both tiers:

   (a) Ich ……… *mochte* ……… nicht in die Schule gehen. (*mögen*)

   (b) Er ……………………… zu Hause helfen. (*müssen*)

   (c) Es ……………………… gestern keine Hausaufgaben. (*geben*)

   (d) Wir ……………………… eine Party zu Hause. (*haben*)

   (e) Ich ……………………… nicht verstehen. (*können*)

   Higher tier only:

   (a) Das Konzert ……… *begann* ……… um 20:30 Uhr. (*beginnen*)

   (b) Ich ……………………… zu Hause. (*bleiben*)

   (c) Mein Freund ……………………… nach Hause. (*kommen*)

   (d) Er ……………………… das Buch. (*lesen*)

   (e) Die Leute ……………………… warten. (*müssen*)

> **Irregular verbs in the perfect tense**
>
> Use the fourth column of the verb tables to check the past participles of irregular verbs. Most end in *-en*. The asterisk (*) tells you that the verb forms its perfect tense with *sein*.

3 Complete each sentence in the perfect tense with the correct part of *haben* or *sein* and the past participle.

   (a) Ich ……… *bin* ……… gestern nicht in die Schule ……… *gegangen* ……… . (*gehen**)

   (b) Was ……………………… du ……………………… ? (*essen*)

   (c) Ich ……………………… meine Handtasche ……………………… . (*finden*)

Had a go ☐   Nearly there ☐   Nailed it! ☐   **Grammar**

Irregular verb tables 2

Refer to the irregular verb tables on page 109 of the Revision Guide to check the verb forms you need to use here.

> **Irregular verbs in the present tense**
>
> Look at the second column of the verb tables to see which, if any, changes happen to the *er / sie / es* form of the verb. Any change will apply to the *du* form too.

1 Circle the correct form of the verb to complete each sentence.
   (a) Ich (**nehme**) / **nimmst** / **nimm** diese Hose.
   (b) Sie **siehst** / **seht** / **sieht** eine Sendung an.
   (c) Er **spreche** / **sprecht** / **spricht** mit meinen Eltern.
   (d) Was **trägst** / **tragt** / **trage** du in der Schule?
   (e) Die Lehrerin **trefft** / **trifft** / **treffe** uns nach der Schule.
   (f) Du **vergesse** / **vergisst** / **vergesst** immer meinen Geburtstag.

> **Irregular verbs in the imperfect tense**
>
> Use the third column of the verb tables to check the imperfect tense *er / sie / es* form. This is also the *ich* form and it acts as the stem to which appropriate endings are added for the other parts of the verb, e.g. *-st* for the *du* form and *-en* for the *wir / Sie / sie* forms.

2 Complete each sentence with the correct imperfect form of the verb in brackets.
   Both tiers:
   (a) Ich .... *wollte* .... ausgehen. (*wollen*)
   (b) Die Lehrerin .... sehr nett. (*sein*)
   (c) Mein Freund .... nicht mitkommen. (*sollen*)
   (d) Ich .... gestern krank. (*sein*)
   (e) Der Lehrer .... nicht glücklich. (*sein*)

   Higher tier only:
   (a) Wir .... *nahmen* .... unseren Hund mit. (*nehmen*)
   (b) Wir .... einen Horrorfilm. (*sehen*)
   (c) Ich .... gut in meinem Zelt. (*schlafen*)
   (d) Wir .... in dem Park. (*sitzen*)
   (e) Mein Freund .... mit dem Manager. (*sprechen*)

> **Irregular verbs in the perfect tense**
>
> Use the fourth column of the verb tables to check the past participle of irregular verbs. Most end in *-en*. The asterisk (*) tells you that the verb forms its perfect tense with *sein*.

3 Complete each sentence in the perfect tense with the correct part of *haben* or *sein* and the past participle.
   (a) Ich .... *bin* .... im Meer .... *geschwommen* .... (*schwimmen**)
   (b) Was .... du .... ? (*nehmen*)
   (c) Er .... nichts .... (*sehen*)
   (d) Ich .... das nicht .... (*vergessen*)

109

Using irregular verbs in different tenses

Grammar — Had a go ☐ Nearly there ☐ Nailed it! ☐

Refer to the irregular verb tables on pages 108 and 109 of the Revision Guide to check the verb forms you need to use here.

1 Complete each sentence with the correct present tense form of the verb in brackets.

   (a) Die Mädchen ......singen...... sehr schön. (*singen*)

   (b) Du .... immer deine Bücher. (*vergessen*)

   (c) Welchen Film .... wir? (*sehen*)

   (d) Mein Bruder .... Horrorfilme. (*mögen*)

   (e) Wann .... dein Bruder nach London? (*fahren*)

   (f) Ich .... keine Schwestern. (*haben*)

2 Circle the correct form of the verb to complete each present tense sentence.

   (a) Wann **beginnst** / **(beginnt)** / **beginnen** der Film?

   (b) Meine Mutter **schreibe** / **schreiben** / **schreibt** viele E-Mails.

   (c) Der Lehrer **spricht** / **sprecht** / **sprechen** gut Deutsch.

   (d) Was **tragt** / **trägst** / **tragen** du heute Abend?

   (e) Die Kinder **trinkt** / **trinken** / **trinkst** oft Milch.

3 Rewrite these present tense sentences in the **perfect** tense.

   Example: Ich **fahre*** nach Österreich. –> Ich **bin** nach Österreich **gefahren**.

   * This reminds you to form the perfect tense of the verb with *sein*!

   (a) Das Konzert **beginnt** spät.
   (b) Was **isst** er in der Pause?
   (c) Ich **gehe*** zu Fuß zur Schule.
   (d) Mein Bruder **gewinnt** einen Preis.
   (e) Wir **bringen** dir ein Geschenk.
   (f) Ich **lese** einen neuen Krimi.
   (g) Wir **helfen** unseren Freunden.
   (h) Ich **laufe*** jeden Morgen am Strand.
   (i) Meine Eltern **kommen*** spät nach Hause.
   (j) Er **trinkt** viel Kaffee.

4 Complete each sentence with the correct imperfect form of the verb in brackets.

   Both tiers:

   (a) Ich .... zu viel Arbeit. (*haben*)

   (b) Man .... nichts sehen. (*können*)

   (c) Er .... eine Stunde auf den Zug warten. (*müssen*)

   Higher tier only:

   (a) Ich .... meinen Kaffee. (*trinken*)

   (b) Wir .... mit dem Arzt. (*sprechen*)

   (c) Er .... ihm ein Geschenk. (*geben*)

Had a go ☐ **Nearly there** ☐ **Nailed it!** ☐ Grammar

Sein and *haben*

Sein and *haben* are perhaps the most useful verbs of all, because they occur so frequently, and also because we use them to form the perfect tense of every other verb. Refer to page 1 and the irregular verb tables on pages 108 and 109 of the Revision Guide for the verb forms you need to use here.

Here are their key forms:			
	present tense *er / sie / es* **form**	**imperfect tense** *er / sie / es* **form**	**past participle**
haben	hat	hatte	gehabt
sein	ist	war	gewesen*

* This means that the verb takes *sein* in the perfect tense. You won't meet *gewesen* in the exam, but it is good to know.

1 Complete the sentences with the correct present tense form of *haben* (a)–(d) or *sein* (e)–(g).
   (a) ....*Hast*.......... du Geschwister?
   (b) Man .... nie genug Zeit.
   (c) Ich .... nächste Woche Geburtstag.
   (d) Die Mädchen .... lange braune Haare.
   (e) Diese Städte .... sehr historisch.
   (f) .... du krank?
   (g) Ich .... in der Tennismannschaft.

2 Complete the sentences with the correct imperfect tense form of *haben* (a)–(d) or *sein* (e)–(g).
   (a) Wir ....*hatten*.......... schönes Wetter.
   (b) Ich .... Angst.
   (c) Die Kinder .... Hunger.
   (d) Er .... Durst.
   (e) Ich .... letzte Woche im Krankenhaus.
   (f) Wo .... deine Freunde?
   (g) Es .... echt spannend!

3 Complete the sentences in the perfect tense with the correct part of *haben* or *sein* plus the past participle.
   (a) Er ....*ist*.......... in der Schweiz ....*gewesen*.......... . (*sein*)
   (b) .... du Angst .... ? (*haben*)
   (c) Wo .... du .... ? (*sein*)
   (d) Meine Noten .... mir immer wichtig .... (*sein*)

Grammar

Had a go ☐ Nearly there ☐ Nailed it! ☐

Modal verbs in the present tense

> Modal verbs need the **infinitive** of another verb to complete their sense.
>
> This infinitive appears at the end of the clause or sentence.
>
> Modal verbs in the **present** tense follow a regular pattern in the plural, but they have some irregular singular forms.
>
> - dürfen – ich / er / sie / es darf
> - können – ich / er / sie / es kann
> - mögen – ich / er / sie / es mag
> - müssen – ich / er / sie / es muss
> - sollen – ich / er / sie / es soll
> - wollen – ich / er / sie / es will

1 Circle the correct form of the modal verb to complete each sentence.

   (a) Mein Bruder **(will)** / **wollen** / **wollt** auf die Uni gehen.

   (b) Wir **soll** / **sollt** / **sollen** die Umwelt schützen.

   (c) Welches Hemd **mag** / **magst** / **mögt** du?

   (d) Hier **dürfen** / **darf** / **darfst** man nicht rauchen.

   (e) Ich **muss** / **musst** / **müssen** bis morgen diese Wörter lernen.

   (f) Wann **kann** / **können** / **könnt** wir dich besuchen?

2 Translate the sentences in Exercise 1 into **English**.

   (a) ....
   (b) ....
   (c) ....
   (d) ....
   (e) ....
   (f) ....

> Modals can also be useful in the **imperfect** tense to say what you had to / wanted to / were able to do. Below are the *ich* forms (which are also the *er / sie / es* forms). Just add the usual endings for the other persons of the verb.
>
> Note that at Foundation tier, you only need to use the **singular forms** of these verbs in the imperfect (*ich / du / er / sie / es / man*).
>
> ich durfte   ich konnte   ich mochte   ich musste   ich sollte   ich wollte

3 Complete each sentence with the imperfect tense form of the verb in brackets.

   Both tiers:

   (a) Ich .... den Jungen nicht. (*mögen*)

   (b) Man .... mehr tun, um anderen zu helfen. (*sollen*)

   (c) Er .... lange auf einen Bus warten. (*müssen*)

   (d) Ich .... kein Wort verstehen. (*können*)

   Higher tier:

   (a) Wir ....*konnten*........ nicht mit dem Zug fahren. (*können*)

   (b) Wohin .... ihr in Urlaub fahren? (*wollen*)

   (c) Leider .... meine Freundinnen nicht mitkommen. (*dürfen*)

Had a go ☐ Nearly there ☐ Nailed it! ☐   **Grammar**

The perfect tense with *haben*

Most verbs form their **perfect** tense with the auxiliary verb *haben*.

The past participle stands at the end of the clause / sentence.

Regular past participles form like this:

- **machen -> mach -> gemacht**
  Ich **habe** einen Sprachkurs **gemacht**.
- Note that if the stem ends in -*d* or -*t*, you should add an extra *e* before the final letter.
  Hast du gearbei**t**et?
- If the verb has an inseparable prefix like **be***nutzen*, no *ge*- is added to the front.
  Ich habe meinen Laptop **be**nutzt.
- If the infinitive ends in -*ieren*, no *ge*- is added to the front, but the past participle ends, as normal, in -*t*.
  Ich habe in Berlin **studiert**.

1 Complete the sentences with the correct part of *haben* and the regular past participle of the verb in brackets.

(a) Ich ......habe...... Golf ......gespielt...... . (*spielen*)

(b) .... er Souvenirs .... ? (*kaufen*)

(c) Wir .... Nachrichten .... (*schicken*)

(d) Meine Freunde .... lange .... (*warten*)

(e) Ich .... in diesem Café .... (*arbeiten*)

(f) Die Klasse .... Mathe .... (*lernen*)

Some verbs have irregular past participles, which often end in *en* rather than the regular -*t*.

Here's a reminder of some common ones you need to know.

essen -> gegess**en**	finden -> gefund**en**	geben -> gegeb**en**
helfen -> gehol**fen**	lesen -> geles**en**	nehmen -> genomm**en**
schreiben -> geschrieb**en**	sprechen -> gesproch**en**	trinken -> getrunk**en**

Use the irregular verb tables on pages 108 and 109 of the Revision Guide to check other irregular past participles. You'll find them in the fourth column.

2 Complete the sentences with an appropriate past participle from the box below.

gegessen	geholfen	gegeben	geschrieben
getroffen	getrunken	~~gelesen~~	gesprochen

(a) Habt ihr diesen spannenden Roman ......gelesen...... ?

(b) Wir haben Pommes und Würste ....

(c) Meine Schwester hat keinen Kaffee ....

(d) Er hat mit der Lehrerin über meine Noten ....

(e) Hast du dem armen Kind .... ?

(f) Ich habe die E-Mail noch nicht ....

(g) Wir haben uns im Park ....

(h) Der Mathelehrer hat uns nochmal viele Hausaufgaben ....

The perfect tense with *sein*

Which verbs form their perfect tense with *sein*?

Verbs which denote:

- movement from A to B, for example:
  ankommen *to arrive*
  fahren *to travel* (note than when *fahren* means 'to drive' and has a direct object (car, etc), it takes *haben* in the perfect tense: Er **hat** sein neues Auto **gefahren**.)
  fliegen *to fly*
  gehen *to go / walk*
  kommen *to come*
  laufen *to run*

- a state
  bleiben *to stay / remain*
  sein *to be*

- a change of state
  werden *to become*

- to happen
  passieren *to happen*
  geschehen *to happen*

> Verbs ending in *-ieren* are all regular but never add *ge-* to the past participle: *Was ist passiert?* What happened?

1 Complete each sentence with the correct part of *sein*.

(a) Ich ………bin……… ins Kino gegangen.

(b) Wann ……………………… du in die Schule gekommen?

(c) Wir ……………………… dahin geflogen.

(d) Mein Freund ……………………… von seinem Fahrrad gefallen.

(e) Die Touristen ……………………… nach Wien gefahren.

(f) Wo ……………………… das passiert?

(g) Viele Leute ……………………… angekommen.

(h) Ich ……………………… dieses Jahr aktiver geworden.

(i) Was ……………………… hier geschehen?

2 Translate these perfect tense sentences into **German**.

(a) Have you been to Berlin? (use *fahren* in the *du* form)

…………………………………………………………………………

(b) We arrived late yesterday evening.

…………………………………………………………………………

(c) I went to the gym this morning.

…………………………………………………………………………

(d) They have been ill.

…………………………………………………………………………

(e) She has become more sporty.

…………………………………………………………………………

Had a go ☐ Nearly there ☐ Nailed it! ☐ **Grammar**

The imperfect tense

> You can use the **imperfect** tense to write about events in the past. Many common verbs are used in the imperfect in spoken language too. Examples include: *war, hatte, musste, konnte, wollte, gab.*
>
> - For **regular** verbs: add *-t* to the stem and then the endings *-e / -ste / -e* in the singular and *-en* for all the plural forms except *ihr*, which ends in *-et*.
>   Ich mach**te** Gartenarbeit.
> - For **irregular** verbs: try to get to know the *er / sie / es* form, which is also the *ich* form. The plural endings are as for regular verbs.
>   Er **hatte** eine Katze.
> - For Foundation tier, the only irregulars you need to know in the imperfect are *haben* and *sein* in full, and just the singular forms of modal verbs like *ich wollte / er musste* and *es gab* (there was / were).

1 Circle the correct imperfect form of these regular verbs to complete each sentence.

(a) Ich **spielten** / **spielte** / **spieltet** gestern Fußball.

(b) Die Schüler **lerntest** / **lernten** / **lernte** viel über das Klima.

(c) Wir **diskutierte** / **diskutierten** / **diskutiertest** über die Umwelt.

(d) Er **kochtest** / **kochte** / **kochten** etwas zu essen.

(e) Meine Tante **malte** / **maltest** / **malten** ein schönes Bild.

(f) Ich **kaufte** / **kauftest** / **kauftet** eine blaue Jacke.

2 Complete the sentences with the correct imperfect form of the irregular verb in brackets.

> Use the irregular verbs tables on pages 108 and 109 of the Revision Guide to check any forms you are not sure of. Look at the third column for the imperfect tense.

Both tiers:

(a) Meine Familie ....war.......... im Urlaub in der Türkei. (*sein*)

(b) Das Kind .... Angst. (*haben*)

(c) Es .... viele Leute in der Stadt. (*geben*)

(d) Ich .... im Bett bleiben. (*müssen*)

(e) Mein Bruder .... nicht ausgehen. (*wollen*)

(f) .... Sie eine gute Reise? (*haben*)

Higher tier:

(a) Das Mädchen .... nach Hause. (*laufen*)

(b) Wann .... der Zug an? (*kommen*)

(c) Wir .... nicht ausgehen. (*können*)

(d) Ich .... im Bett. (*bleiben*)

(e) Meine Freunde .... Fastfood. (*essen*)

(f) Wir .... jeden Morgen. (*schwimmen*)

(g) Ich .... spät nach Hause. (*gehen*)

(h) Die Schülerin .... mir ein Geschenk. (*geben*)

(i) Er .... mit dem Auto in die Berge. (*fahren*)

Grammar — Had a go ☐ Nearly there ☐ Nailed it! ☐

The future tense

The correct part of *werden* + *infinitive*			
ich	werde	in die Stadt	gehen
du	wirst	nicht genug Zeit	haben
er / sie / es	wird	seinem Freund	helfen
wir	werden	nicht mit dem Flugzeug	fliegen
ihr	werdet	heute Basketball	spielen
Sie	werden	in diesem Restaurant	essen
sie	werden	in den Sommerferien	wandern

1. Complete each sentence with the correct part of *werden*.

    (a) Was .... wirst .... du nach den Prüfungen machen?

    (b) Ich .... im September Fremdsprachen lernen.

    (c) Meine Schwester .... einen Job in London suchen.

    (d) Wir .... nächstes Jahr nicht in den Urlaub fahren.

    (e) Meine Freundinnen .... am Samstag tanzen gehen.

2. Rewrite these jumbled sentences in the correct order, starting with the words in **bold**.

    (a) gehen / **Mein Freund** / auf die Uni / im Oktober / wird

    (b) werde / sein / **Ich denke** / ich / Tierärztin

    (c) haben / nächstes Jahr / eine Party / werden / **Wir**

    (d) Wasser / nicht / in der Zukunft / genug / **Es wird** / geben

    (e) unsere Welt / **Flugzeuge** / weiter / zerstören / werden

    > Remember that you can use a **future time marker** (e.g. *nächste Woche, in der Zukunft, morgen, in den Ferien*) and a **present** tense verb to indicate a future time frame.
    > Nächsten Samstag arbeite ich in einem Restaurant.
    > Another alternative is to use *ich will* (I want to) or *ich möchte* (I would like to).
    > All these expressions need an infinitive at the end.

3. Translate these sentences into **English**, each time referring to the future.

    (a) Nächsten September gehe ich in die Oberstufe.

    ....

    (b) Heute Abend wollen wir mit meinen Großeltern essen.

    ....

    (c) In der Zukunft heirate ich bestimmt nicht.

    ....

4. Translate these sentences into **German**.

    (a) In the future, I would like to work with animals. ....

    (b) I want to be an actor. ....

    (c) Next week, I want to buy some new clothes. ....

Had a go ☐ **Nearly there** ☐ **Nailed it!** ☐

Grammar

The conditional

> The structure is the same as for the future tense, except that you use *würde* instead of *werde*.
>
> Ich würde gerne ins Ausland fahren.
> Ich würde lieber Geld verdienen.
> Ich würde am liebsten ein Studium machen.
>
> You can use *gern / lieber / am liebsten* (I would like / I would prefer / best of all I would like …) to intensify your idea.

1 Rewrite these future tense sentences in the conditional.

(a) Ich werde Geschichte studieren. ....

(b) Mein Bruder wird eine Lehre machen. ....

(c) Unsere Lehrerin wird nicht zufrieden sein. ....

(d) Was werden sie machen? ....

(e) Vielleicht werde ich die Schule verlassen. ....

> A full conditional sentence often uses a ***wenn*** clause to say what you would do **if** …
>
> The verb in the *wenn* clause can either be a **conditional** or the **imperfect subjunctive** form, which has the same meaning but often sounds more natural.
>
> | conditional | imperfect subjunctive alternative | meaning |
> |---|---|---|
> | Ich würde … haben | Ich hätte | *I would have* |
> | Wir würden … können | Wir könnten | *We would be able to* |
> | Es würde … sein | Es wäre | *It would be* |
> | Wir würden … mögen | Wir möchten | *We would like* |
>
> Here are some useful examples of imperfect subjunctives for you to use and learn, although many of them are not required in the AQA specification:
>
> Wenn ich … **dürfte**, würde ich …   *If I was allowed to …. I would …*
> Wenn es … **gäbe**, würde ich …   *If there was / were …, I would …*
> Wenn ich … **hätte**, würde ich…   *If I had …, I would …*
> Wenn ich … **könnte**, würde ich …   *If I could …, I would …*
> Wenn ich … **wäre**, würde ich …   *If I was …, I would …*
>
> Note: *möchten* is also needed for Foundation tier.

2 Translate these conditional sentences into **English**.

(a) Ich würde die Schule sofort verlassen, wenn ich dürfte.

....

(b) Was würde er machen, wenn er reich wäre?

....

(c) Ich würde einen langen Urlaub auf einer Insel verbringen.

....

(d) Wenn er könnte, würde mein Bruder mit seiner Freundin zusammenleben.

....

(e) Wenn ich Schuldirektor wäre, gäbe es keine Hausaufgaben mehr.

....

Paper 1: Listening (Foundation)

Had a go ☐ Nearly there ☐ Nailed it! ☐

AQA publishes official Sample Assessment Material on its website. This test has been written to help you practise what you have learned across the four skills and may not be representative of a real exam paper.

School subjects

Track 120

Four Austrian friends are discussing school subjects.

Which subject does each person mention? Write the correct letter in the box.

A	Art	C	English	E	Maths
B	Biology	D	French	F	Technology

1 Alex ☐ **(1 mark)**   2 Sofia ☐ **(1 mark)**
3 Yusuf ☐ **(1 mark)**   4 Yasmin ☐ **(1 mark)**

Eating habits

Track 121

You hear two German girls talking about food. What do they like to eat and why?

Write the correct **letter** for the food in the **What?** box.

Write the correct **number** for the reason in the **Why?** box.

What?

A	cheese
B	chicken
C	fruit
D	vegetables

Why?

1	delicious
2	fresh
3	healthy
4	sweet

		What?	Why?	
5	Pamela	☐	☐	(2 marks)
6	Nadia	☐	☐	(2 marks)

Relationships

Track 122

Two German boys are talking about their girlfriends. What do they think of their relationships?

Write **P** for a **positive** opinion

N for a **negative** opinion

P+N for a **positive and negative** opinion.

Answer both parts of question 7.

7.1 Sascha ☐ **(1 mark)**   7.2 Thomas ☐ **(1 mark)**

Social media

Track 123

You hear a discussion on Swiss radio about social media.

Choose the correct answer and write the letter in each box.

Answer all parts of question 8.

8.1 What does the male speaker think is the main problem?

A	Sharing photos.
B	Sharing personal information.
C	Sharing passwords.

☐

8.2 What does the female speaker see as a positive aspect?

A	Talking about problems.
B	Finding new friends.
C	Making social arrangements.

☐

8.3 What does she say young people must avoid doing?

A	Sharing photos with strangers.
B	Arranging to meet strangers.
C	Accepting strangers as online friends.

☐

(3 marks)

Had a go ☐ **Nearly there** ☐ **Nailed it!** ☐   **Practice papers**

A rock star

You hear an interview with German rock musician Benno Venus.

What does he say? Write the correct letter in each box.

Answer both parts of question 9.

9.1 As a teenager Benno …

A	had singing lessons.
B	played solo concerts.
C	wrote some songs.

9.2 His life has changed since he …

A	appeared on television.
B	had a number one hit.
C	formed a new band.

(2 marks)

Jobs

Three Swiss friends are talking about jobs.

Write **P** if they are talking about a job in the past

N if they are talking about a job now

F if they are talking about a job in the future.

Answer all parts of question 10.

10.1 Elif ☐ **(1 mark)**   10.2 Ben ☐ **(1 mark)**   10.3 Robin ☐ **(1 mark)**

The environment

You hear a Swiss podcast about the environment.

Choose the correct answer and write the letter in each box.

Answer all parts of question 11.

11.1 Which area is the speaker concerned about?

A	The coast.
B	The forest.
C	The mountains.

11.2 What is the main cause of the problem in this area?

A	The aeroplanes.
B	The hikers.
C	The motorists.

11.3 Which group of people does she mention?

A	The locals.
B	The tourists.
C	The young people.

11.4 What does she say about the effect of littering?

A	It discourages visitors.
B	It endangers wildlife.
C	It pollutes rivers.

(4 marks)

School life

You hear two Austrian students talking about their school life.

Complete the sentences in **English**. Write **one** word in each space.

Example: The biggest problem for me is ….*homework*…. because I find it ….*difficult*….

12 I like my school because the teachers are …………………………… .

They …………………………… when I don't understand something.   **(2 marks)**

13 I hate the …………………………… .

They are cold and …………………………… in winter.   **(2 marks)**

119

Practice papers

Had a go ☐ Nearly there ☐ Nailed it! ☐

Holidays

Four German friends are talking about how they like to spend the holidays.

What activity does each person like to do on holiday?

Write the correct letter in the box.

A	cycling	C	hiking	E	sailing
B	gardening	D	reading	F	seeing the sights

14 Paul ☐ **(1 mark)**   **15** Anke ☐ **(1 mark)**

16 Lukas ☐ **(1 mark)**   **17** Jana ☐ **(1 mark)**

A celebration

Finn is describing a family celebration.

Answer the questions in **English**.

Answer both parts of question 18.

18.1 Who organised the wedding?

.... **(1 mark)**

18.2 What did the bride wear?

.... **(1 mark)**

Dictation

You will now hear four short sentences.

Listen carefully and using your knowledge of German sounds, write down in **German** exactly what you hear for each sentence.

You will hear each sentence **three** times: the first time as a full sentence, the second time in short sections and the third time again as a full sentence.

Sentence 1

....

....

Sentence 2

....

....

Sentence 3

....

....

Sentence 4

....

....

(8 marks)

TOTAL FOR PAPER = 40 MARKS

Had a go ☐ Nearly there ☐ Nailed it! ☐

Practice papers

Paper 2: Speaking (Foundation)

Role play

1 You are talking to your German friend.

Listen to the recording of the teacher's part. The teacher will play the part of your friend and will speak first.

You should address your friend as *du*.

When you see this – **?** – you will have to ask a question.

> **In order to score full marks, you must include a verb in your response to each task.**
> 1 Say one thing you do at the weekend.
> 2 Say how often you play sport.
> ?3 Ask your friend a question about watching television.
> 4 Say what you think of films at the cinema.
> 5 Give **one** opinion of your local cinema.

(10 marks)

Reading aloud

2 Read aloud the following text in **German**.

> Ich habe viele Freunde und Freundinnen.
> Wir verstehen uns immer gut und streiten selten.
> Meine beste Freundin ist nett und lustig.
> Am Samstag gehe ich in der Stadt einkaufen.
> Ich kaufe am liebsten neue Kleidung.

Now listen to the recording of four questions in **German** that relate to the topic of **Identity and relationships with others**.

In order to score the highest marks, you must try to **answer all four questions as fully as you can**.

(15 marks)

Photo card

3 Look at the two photos as part of your preparation. Make as many notes as you want on an Additional Answer Sheet for use during the test. You will be asked about the content of these photos by your teacher. The recommended time is approximately **one minute**. **You must say at least one thing about each photo**. After you have spoken about the content of the photos, you will then be asked questions related to **any** of the topics within the theme of **People and lifestyle**.

Photo 1

Photo 2

(25 marks)

TOTAL FOR PAPER = 50 MARKS

Paper 3: Reading (Foundation)

Practice papers — Had a go ☐ Nearly there ☐ Nailed it! ☐

SECTION A

School subjects

Read these comments by four Swiss teenagers on an internet forum.

> **Arda:** Ich mag Wissenschaft. Die Lehrerin ist gut.
>
> **Leonie:** Mein Lieblingsfach ist Kunst. Ich finde die Stunden entspannend.
>
> **Matteo:** Ich lerne nicht gern Fremdsprachen.
>
> **Layla:** Erdkunde finde ich sehr interessant.

Which subject does each person mention?

Write the correct letter in each box.

A	Art	C	History	E	Science
B	Geography	D	Languages	F	Technology

1 Arda ☐ (1 mark)

2 Leonie ☐ (1 mark)

3 Matteo ☐ (1 mark)

4 Layla ☐ (1 mark)

Sport

Read these comments from three German students about sport.

> **Alex:** Mannschaftssport ist nichts für mich, aber ich bin gern aktiv und gehe samstags wandern.
>
> **Finn:** Ich gehe dreimal die Woche ins Fitness-Studio, wo ich einen Tanzkurs mache. Das baut Muskeln auf und macht mich stark.
>
> **Toni:** Jeden Morgen trainiere ich in meinem Schwimmverein. Das ist schwer, denn ich muss früh aufstehen.

Match the correct person with each of the following questions.

Write **A** for **Alex**

F for **Finn**

T for **Toni**.

Write the correct letter in each box.

5 Who has an early start every day? ☐ (1 mark)

6 Who is not keen on team sports? ☐ (1 mark)

7 Who wants to build strength? ☐ (1 mark)

8 Who attends a class? ☐ (1 mark)

9 Who likes hiking? ☐ (1 mark)

10 Who is a member of a club? ☐ (1 mark)

Had a go ☐ **Nearly there** ☐ **Nailed it!** ☐   **Practice papers**

Past holidays

You read these comments about recent holidays.

> **Yusuf:** Wir waren auf einem Campingplatz in Norddeutschland. Der Platz war groß und hatte schöne Bäume, aber die Toiletten waren gar nicht sauber.
>
> **Fatima:** Ich bin zu Ostern nach Frankreich gefahren. Mein Hotel in Paris war schmutzig und laut, aber auch sehr teuer.
>
> **Magda:** Ich war mit meiner Familie in einer Ferienwohnung. Die Zimmer waren klein, aber schön, und wir waren direkt am Strand. Das war praktisch.
>
> **Paul:** Mein Aktivurlaub in den Bergen war ein Traum. Die Landschaft war ideal zum Wandern. Die **Unterkunft** war auch sehr bequem: ich hatte ein ruhiges Schlafzimmer mit Badezimmer und einer kleinen Küche.

What did these people think about their holidays?

Write **P** for a **positive** opinion

N for a **negative** opinion

P+N for a **positive** and **negative** opinion.

Write the correct letter in each box.

11 Yusuf ☐ **(1 mark)**   **12** Fatima ☐ **(1 mark)**

13 Magda ☐ **(1 mark)**   **14** Paul ☐ **(1 mark)**

15 Read the last paragraph again. What does **Unterkunft** mean?

Write the correct letter in the box.

| A | accommodation | B | route | C | transport |

☐ **(1 mark)**

Celebrations

You read Leon's online comments about celebrations.

> Wenn jemand bei uns Geburtstag hat, feiern wir immer zusammen. Normalerweise kochen wir ein Festessen zu Hause und laden die ganze Familie ein. Das macht immer Spaß, und ich mag es, Zeit mit meinen Großeltern zu verbringen.
>
> Zu Ostern gehen wir in die Kirche und gehen danach an der Küste spazieren, wenn es nicht zu kalt ist. An Silvester gibt es jedes Jahr auf unserer Straße eine Party, wo alle Nachbarn etwas kochen und es mitbringen. Es gibt Musik und Tanzen, und alle genießen einen tollen Abend.

Complete these sentences. Write the letter for the correct option in each box.

16 Leon's family celebrates birthdays …

A	at his grandparents' house.
B	at home.
C	in a restaurant.

☐ **(1 mark)**

17 Leon finds these occasions …

A	boring.
B	fun.
C	tiring.

☐ **(1 mark)**

18 At Easter, they …

A	go out for lunch.
B	go swimming.
C	go to church.

☐ **(1 mark)**

19 There is a street party on …

A	Christmas Day.
B	New Year's Day.
C	New Year's Eve.

☐ **(1 mark)**

Practice papers

Had a go ☐ Nearly there ☐ Nailed it! ☐

House and home

You read Ahmad's post online.

> Ich arbeite jetzt als Manager eines italienischen Restaurants in Köln und habe eine Dreizimmerwohnung über dem Restaurant, wo ich mit meiner Frau und unserem Kind wohne.
>
> Als Kind und Jugendlicher war ich in Syrien*, wo das Leben sehr gefährlich war. Damals hat unsere Familie in einem Zimmer bei meinen Großeltern gelebt.
>
> In der Zukunft hoffen wir, unser eigenes Haus zu haben. Wir möchten einen Garten haben, wo unser Sohn spielen kann.

* *Syrien* – Syria

Write **P** for a type of accommodation he had in the **past**

N for a type of accommodation he has **now**

F for a type of accommodation he wants in the **future**.

Write the correct letter in each box.

Answer all parts of question 20.

20.1 A house ☐ **(1 mark)**   20.2 A room ☐ **(1 mark)**   20.3 A flat ☐ **(1 mark)**

A healthy lifestyle

Read Julian's blog about his lifestyle.

> Ich weiß, dass ich gesünder leben soll. Ich versuche, mich jeden Tag zu bewegen, aber das ist nicht immer einfach, denn ich habe so viele Hausaufgaben und muss auch meiner Mutter im Haus helfen, weil sie lange Arbeitszeiten hat. Ich gehe jetzt täglich zu Fuß zur Schule, um meine Fitness zu verbessern, und samstags spiele ich ab und zu Fußball mit meinen Freunden. Leider ist das nicht immer möglich, weil ich für die Familie einkaufen gehe. Wenn mein kleiner Bruder ein bisschen älter ist, kann er vielleicht mit mir Sport machen.

Answer the following questions in **English**.

21 Why does Julian find it difficult to find time to exercise? Give **two** details.   **(2 marks)**

(i) ....

(ii) ....

22 What does he do every day to improve his fitness level?   **(1 mark)**

....

23 Why can he not always play football on Saturdays?   **(1 mark)**

....

24 What does he think might happen in the future?   **(1 mark)**

....

Had a go ☐ Nearly there ☐ Nailed it! ☐   **Practice papers**

Headlines

You see these German newspaper headlines online.

A	Immer mehr Arbeitslose in Hamburg	D	Neues Schulgebäude in Berlin
B	Extreme Temperaturen in Spanien	E	Bekannter Musiker tot gefunden
C	Gefahren der Technologie für Jugendliche	F	Vögel sterben am Strand

Which headline matches each topic?

Write the correct letter in each box.

25 Education matters ☐ **(1 mark)**   **26** Death of a star ☐ **(1 mark)**

27 Climate change ☐ **(1 mark)**   **28** Unemployment figures ☐ **(1 mark)**

A German actress

You read this article about the German actress, Franka Potente.

> Franka Potente ist 1974 in Dülmen* geboren.
>
> Mit 17 Jahren war sie ein Jahr als Austauschschülerin** in Texas. Sie machte in Dülmen das Abitur und 1994 hat sie eine Schauspielerausbildung begonnen.
>
> Ihre erste Rolle in einem deutschen Spielfilm hatte sie 1995. Für diese Rolle hat sie den Preis als beste junge Schauspielerin gewonnen. 1998 spielte sie die Starrolle in dem erfolgreichen Actionthriller „Lola rennt".
>
> Franka ist auch **Schriftstellerin** und hat drei Bücher geschrieben. Ihr erstes Buch heißt „Los Angeles – Berlin. Ein Jahr".

* *Dülmen* – a town in Germany

** *Austauschschülerin* – exchange student

Answer the following questions in **English**.

29 What age was Franka when she first went to the United States?

.... **(1 mark)**

30 What did she do in 1994?

.... **(1 mark)**

31 What was her first award?

.... **(1 mark)**

32 In what sort of film did she have her first starring role?

.... **(1 mark)**

33 Read the last paragraph again. What does **Schriftstellerin** mean?

Write the correct letter in the box.

A	author
B	composer
C	trainer

☐ **(1 mark)**

125

Practice papers

Had a go ☐ Nearly there ☐ Nailed it! ☐

Social media

Read this extract from an advice booklet for young people.

> Die sozialen Medien sind ein wunderbarer Ort für junge Leute! Man kann sehr einfach mit anderen in Kontakt bleiben, Spaß haben und neue Dinge lernen. Jugendliche können Nachrichten schicken und Fotos und Videos mit Freunden teilen. So weit, so gut!
>
> Man muss aber auch an seine Sicherheit denken. Es gibt ein Risiko, wenn man online mit Personen spricht, die man nicht kennt. Solche Leute sind nicht immer so, wie sie scheinen. Man soll nie private Fotos mit Fremden teilen, wenn man diese Bilder nicht überall im Internet sehen will. Vergessen Sie nicht, dass einige Menschen ehrlich und andere böse und unehrlich sein können.

What advantages and dangers of social media are mentioned?

Write the correct **letters** for **two** advantages in the boxes.

Write the correct **numbers** for **two** dangers in the boxes.

Advantages

A	interesting adverts
B	easy communication
C	educational element
D	top fashion tips

Dangers

1	costs of gaming
2	fake news
3	misuse of private images
4	strangers as online friends

34 Advantages ☐ ☐ (2 marks)

35 Dangers ☐ ☐ (2 marks)

SECTION B

Translation into English

36 Translate these sentences into **English**.

Ich höre gern Musik.

.... (2 marks)

Meine Schwester geht am Samstag einkaufen.

.... (2 marks)

Ich muss jeden Tag zwei Stunden Hausaufgaben machen.

.... (2 marks)

Im Juli fahren wir immer in den Urlaub nach Frankreich.

.... (2 marks)

Gestern habe ich in der Deutschstunde viel gelernt.

.... (2 marks)

TOTAL FOR PAPER = 50 MARKS

Had a go ☐ Nearly there ☐ Nailed it! ☐   **Practice papers**

Paper 4: Writing (Foundation)

In the real exam, you will write your answers on the question paper. Here, you will need to write some of the answers on your own paper.

SECTION A

1 You see this photo on social media. What is in this photo? Write **five** sentences in **German**.

1.1 .... **(2 marks)**
1.2 .... **(2 marks)**
1.3 .... **(2 marks)**
1.4 .... **(2 marks)**
1.5 .... **(2 marks)**

2 Write to a German friend about how you spend your free time. Write approximately **50** words in **German**. You must write something about each bullet point.

Mention:
- sport
- going out
- shopping
- activities with friends
- activities at home.

(10 marks)

3 Using your knowledge of grammar, complete the following sentences in **German**. Choose the correct German word from the three options in the grid. Write the correct **word** in the space, as shown in the example below.

Example:

Ich ......*gehe*...... in die Stadt.

geht	gehe	gehen

3.1 Mein Freund .... eine Katze.

hast	habe	hat

3.2 .... kaufe manchmal Kuchen.

Ich	Er	Du

3.3 Sie haben ein .... Auto.

neue	neuer	neues

3.4 Die Schule .... sehr modern.

ist	seid	sind

3.5 .... Junge ist alter als ich.

Das	Die	Der

(5 marks)

4 Translate the following sentences into **German**.

This year, I am fifteen years old.
We live in a small town.
I think maths is a difficult subject.
She wants to go shopping today after school.
Last Saturday, we went to a concert.

(10 marks)

SECTION B

A letter

5 Choose either Question 5(a) or Question 5(b).

(a) Write a letter to your Swiss friend about your lifestyle. You **must** include the following points: • how you keep fit and healthy • what you ate and drank yesterday • how you will relax this evening.	(b) Write a letter to a German friend about technology. You **must** include the following points: • how you use your mobile phone • what you have done recently on the internet • how you will use social media in the future.

Write your answer in **German**. You should aim to write approximately **90** words. **(15 marks)**

TOTAL FOR PAPER = 50 MARKS

Paper 1: Listening (Higher)

AQA publishes official Sample Assessment Material on its website. This test has been written to help you practise what you have learned across the four skills and may not be representative of a real exam paper.

A rock star

You hear an interview with German rock musician Benno Venus.

What does he say?

Choose the correct answer and write the letter in each box.

Answer both parts of question 1.

1.1 As a teenager Benno …

A	had singing lessons.
B	played solo concerts.
C	wrote some songs.

1.2 His life has changed since he …

A	appeared on television.
B	had a number one hit.
C	formed a new band.

(2 marks)

The environment

You hear a Swiss podcast about the environment.

Choose the correct answer and write the letter in the box.

Answer all parts of question 2.

2.1 Which area is the speaker concerned about?

A	The coast.
B	The forest.
C	The mountains.

2.2 What is the main cause of the problem in this area?

A	The aeroplanes.
B	The hikers.
C	The motorists.

2.3 Which group of people does she mention?

A	The locals.
B	The tourists.
C	The young people.

2.4 What does she say about the effect of littering?

A	It discourages visitors.
B	It endangers wildlife.
C	It pollutes rivers.

(4 marks)

Holidays

Four German friends are talking about how they like to spend the holidays.

What does each person like to do on holiday?

Write the correct letter in the box.

A	cycling	D	reading
B	gardening	E	sailing
C	hiking	F	seeing the sights

3 Paul   (1 mark)

4 Anke   (1 mark)

5 Lukas   (1 mark)

6 Jana   (1 mark)

Had a go ☐ **Nearly there** ☐ **Nailed it!** ☐   **Practice papers**

A celebration

Finn is describing a family celebration.

Answer the question in **English**.

Answer both parts of question 7.

7.1 Who organised the wedding?

.... (1 mark)

7.2 What did the bride wear?

.... (1 mark)

Daily life

Some Austrians are talking about their daily lives.

What opinions do they have about their daily lives?

Write **P** for a **positive** opinion

    N for a **negative** opinion

    P+N for a **positive and negative** opinion.

8 Lara ☐ (1 mark)

9 Jonas ☐ (1 mark)

10 Brigitte ☐ (1 mark)

11 Martin ☐ (1 mark)

Weekend activities

Two German friends are talking about weekend activities.

Write the correct **number** for the activity they mention.

Write the correct **letter** for when they do it.

Activity	
1	climbing
2	drawing
3	football
4	swimming

When	
P	Past
N	Now
F	Future

12 Activity ☐ When ☐ (2 marks)

13 Activity ☐ When ☐ (2 marks)

Practice papers

Had a go ☐ Nearly there ☐ Nailed it! ☐

Relationships

Emily talks about her relationships with her family.

Complete the sentences in **English**.

Write **one** word in each space.

Example: Emily finds her ….*mother*…. great because she is always ….*patient*…… .

14 Emily doesn't get on so well with her ………………… because he is sometimes ……………… . (2 marks)

15 Emily thinks her stepsister is ………………… because she never ………………… . (2 marks)

16 Emily finds it ………………… that she has to clean up the ………………… . (2 marks)

Future plans

You hear two German teenagers talking about future plans.

What do they say?

Write **A** if only statement **A** is correct

B if only statement **B** is correct

A+B if both statements **A** and **B** are correct.

17 Finn …

| A | plans to go to university. |
| B | thinks it is important to be well paid. |

(1 mark)

18 Mila …

| A | wants to work as a doctor. |
| B | would like to do voluntary work. |

(1 mark)

19 Samira …

| A | plans to have a gap year. |
| B | wants to go to Spain and Italy. |

(1 mark)

Celebrity culture

Matteo and Elif are describing their favourite stars.

Answer the questions in **English**.

Answer all parts of question 20.

20.1 What does Matteo admire about his role model? Give **two** details.

……

…… (2 marks)

20.2 What does this star say about being gay?

…… (1 mark)

20.3 What first impressed Elif about her favourite celebrity? Give **two** details.

……

…… (2 marks)

Had a go ☐ Nearly there ☐ Nailed it! ☐   Practice papers

Health issues

You hear the start of a radio programme about young people's health.

Which **three** topics will be dealt with in the programme?

Write the correct letter in each box.

| A | diet | B | exercise | C | hydration | D | sleep | E | smoking |

21 ☐ (1 mark)

22 ☐ (1 mark)

23 ☐ (1 mark)

A place of interest in Berlin

You hear this podcast about a Berlin tourist attraction.

Answer the questions in **English**.

Answer all parts of question 24.

24.1 What is unusual about the location of the museums?

.... (1 mark)

24.2 What can visitors see there? Give **one** detail.

.... (1 mark)

24.3 Why is a guided visit a good idea?

.... (1 mark)

Dictation

You will now hear five short sentences.

Listen carefully and using your knowledge of German sounds, write down in **German** exactly what you hear for each sentence.

You will hear each sentence **three** times: the first time as a full sentence, the second time in short sections and the third time again as a full sentence.

Use your knowledge of German sounds and grammar to make sure that what you have written makes sense. Check carefully that your spelling is accurate.

Sentence 1

....

Sentence 2

....

Sentence 3

....

Sentence 4

....

Sentence 5

.... **(10 marks)**

TOTAL FOR PAPER = 50 MARKS

Practice papers Had a go ☐ Nearly there ☐ Nailed it! ☐

Paper 2: Speaking (Higher)

Role play

1 You are talking to your Austrian friend.

Listen to the recording of the teacher's part. The teacher will play the part of your friend and will speak first.

You should address your friend as *du*.

When you see this – ? – you will have to ask a question.

> **In order to score full marks, you must include at least one verb in your response to each task.**
> 1 Say what you think of your town or village. (Give **one** opinion and **one** reason.)
> ?2 Ask your friend a question about where they live.
> 3 Say what there is for tourists in your area.
> 4 Say what the shops are like in your town or village.
> 5 Say what you will do in town this weekend.

(10 marks)

Reading aloud

2 Read aloud the following text in **German**.

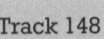

> Ich gehe auf ein großes Gymnasium in der Stadt.
> Das Hauptgebäude ist alt, aber die Klassenzimmer und die Kantine sind modern.
> Alle Schüler müssen zwei Fremdsprachen lernen, was ich toll finde.
> Meine Lieblingsfächer sind Spanisch und Englisch, denn ich finde sie wichtig.
> In der Zukunft möchte ich gern im Ausland arbeiten.

(5 marks)

Now listen to the recording of four questions in **German** that relate to the topic of **Education and work**. In order to score the highest marks, you must try to **answer all four questions as fully as you can.** (10 marks)

Photo card

3 Look at the two photos as part of your preparation. Make as many notes as you want on an Additional Answer Sheet for use during the test. You will be asked about the content of these photos by your teacher. The recommended time is approximately **one and a half minutes**. **You must say at least one thing about each photo.** After you have spoken about the content of the photos, you will then be asked questions related to **any** of the topics within the theme of **Communication and the world around us**. (25 marks)

Photo 1

Photo 2

TOTAL FOR PAPER = 50 MARKS

Had a go ☐ Nearly there ☐ Nailed it! ☐   **Practice papers**

Paper 3: Reading (Higher)

SECTION A

Social media

Read this extract from an advice booklet for young people.

> Die sozialen Medien sind ein wunderbarer Ort für junge Leute! Man kann sehr einfach mit anderen in Kontakt bleiben, Spaß haben und neue Dinge lernen. Jugendliche können Nachrichten schicken und Fotos und Videos mit Freunden teilen. So weit, so gut!
>
> Man muss auch an seine Sicherheit denken. Es gibt ein Risiko, wenn man online mit Personen spricht, die man nicht kennt. Solche Leute sind nicht immer so, wie sie scheinen. Man sollte nie private Fotos mit Fremden teilen – sonst können diese Bilder überall im Internet sein. Vergessen Sie nicht, dass einige Menschen ehrlich und andere böse und unehrlich sein können.

What advantages and dangers of social media are mentioned?

Write the correct **letters** for **two** advantages in the boxes.

Write the correct **numbers** for **two** dangers in the boxes.

Advantages

A	interesting adverts
B	easy communication
C	educational element
D	top fashion tips

Dangers

1	costs of gaming
2	fake news
3	misuse of private images
4	strangers as online friends

1 Advantages ☐ ☐   (2 marks)

2 Dangers   ☐ ☐   (2 marks)

Headlines

You see these German newspaper headlines online.

A	Immer mehr Arbeitslose in Hamburg
B	Extreme Temperaturen in Spanien
C	Gefahren der Technologie für Jugendliche
D	Neues Gymnasium in Berlin
E	Bekannter Musiker tot gefunden
F	Vögel sterben am Strand

Which headline matches each topic?

Write the correct letter in each box.

3 Education matters   ☐   (1 mark)

4 Death of a star   ☐   (1 mark)

5 Climate change   ☐   (1 mark)

6 Unemployment figures   ☐   (1 mark)

Practice papers — Had a go ☐ Nearly there ☐ Nailed it! ☐

A German actress

You read this article about the German actress, Franka Potente.

> Franka Potente ist 1974 in Dülmen* geboren.
>
> Mit 17 Jahren war sie ein Jahr als Austauschschülerin in Texas. 1994 machte sie in Dülmen das Abitur und begann eine Schauspielerausbildung. Sie hat die Ausbildung nach zwei Jahren abgebrochen**, um wieder nach Amerika zu fliegen.
>
> Ihre erste Rolle in einem deutschen Spielfilm war hatte sie 1995. Für diese Rolle hat sie den Preis als beste junge Schauspielerin gewonnen. 1998 spielte sie die Starrolle in dem erfolgreichen Actionthriller „Lola rennt".
>
> Franka ist auch **Schriftstellerin** und hat drei Bücher geschrieben. Ihr erstes Buch heißt „Los Angeles – Berlin. Ein Jahr".

* *Dülmen* – a town in Germany   ** *abbrechen* – to break off / stop

Answer the following questions in **English.**

7 What age was Franka when she first went to the United States?

.... **(1 mark)**

8 What was her first award? .... **(1 mark)**

9 In what sort of film did she have her first starring role? .... **(1 mark)**

10 Read the last paragraph again. What does **Schriftstellerin** mean?

   Write the correct letter in the box.

   | A | author | B | composer | C | trainer |

   ☐ **(1 mark)**

Future plans

You read these online posts about plans for the future.

> **Hanna:** Ich mache mir manchmal Sorgen um die Zukunft, denn ich weiß noch nicht, was ich machen möchte – und viele meiner Freunde haben schon feste Pläne. Ich denke, ich werde vielleicht ein Auslandsjahr machen, wo ich Zeit in England oder in Amerika verbringen werde, um meine Sprachkenntnisse zu verbessern. Das wird toll sein.
>
> **Mika:** Meine Zukunftspläne sind ganz klar, und ich freue mich sehr darauf. Ich werde ein Studium hier in Berlin machen und danach als Anwältin arbeiten. Es ist wichtig für mich, einen interessanten Beruf zu haben und gut zu verdienen.
>
> **Felix:** Meine Noten sind im Moment nicht sehr gut, und ich habe Angst, ich werde das Abitur nicht bestehen. Ich wollte immer Arzt werden, aber ich denke jetzt, dass ich das nie schaffen werde.

How does each person feel about their future prospects?

Write **P** for a **positive** opinion

   N for a **negative** opinion

   P+N for a **positive** and **negative** opinion.

Write the correct letter in each box.

11 Hanna ☐ **(1 mark)**   12 Mika ☐ **(1 mark)**   13 Felix ☐ **(1 mark)**

Had a go ☐ **Nearly there** ☐ **Nailed it!** ☐

Practice papers

Answer the following question in **English.**

14 Why does Hanna want to spend time in England or in the USA?

.... **(1 mark)**

May Day
You read an article about May Day.

> Der erste Mai ist ein nationaler Feiertag. Man nennt ihn auch den Tag der Arbeit oder auch Maifeiertag. Er ist in Deutschland, Österreich, in Teilen der Schweiz und in vielen anderen Ländern ein gesetzlicher* Feiertag. Die meisten Schulen und Geschäfte sind an diesem Tag geschlossen.
>
> Der Maifeiertag hat eine lange Tradition und ist eng mit Arbeitsbedingungen verbunden**. In einigen Großstädten gibt es Demonstrationen, und der Kampf für familienfreundliche Arbeitszeiten und höhere Gehälter spielt eine wichtige Rolle. Die meisten Leute genießen einfach einen Tag ohne Arbeit, um auf dem Land zu wandern und Freizeit mit Freunden zu verbringen.

* *gesetzlich* – official

** *verbunden mit* – connected with

Complete the sentences. Write the letter for the correct option in each box.

15 On May Day most shops are …

A	closed.
B	open all day.
C	open in the morning.

(1 mark)

16 The May Day celebration is …

A	a recent development.
B	an old tradition.
C	a religious occasion.

(1 mark)

17 Demonstrations are held to …

A	celebrate business success.
B	fight for better working conditions.
C	protest against unemployment.

(1 mark)

18 Most people use the day to …

A	catch up on work.
B	enjoy themselves.
C	join the protests.

(1 mark)

A theme park
You read this advert for a theme park.

> Hier ist seit 18 Jahren ein beliebter österreichischer Urlaubsort für die Familie, der in ganz Europa bekannt ist! Der Freizeitpark liegt in einer wunderschönen Naturlandschaft und bietet nicht nur für Kinder, sondern für alle Besucher – egal welchen Alters – Bewegung, Spiel und Spaß.
>
> Mit Hunderten von Attraktionen in unserem Naturerlebnis*park können Kinder ab zwölf Jahren alles unabhängig entdecken – und finden immer etwas Schönes zu tun. Besuchen Sie zum Beispiel unseren riesigen Wasserspielplatz! (Neu seit 2023.)
>
> Wenn Sie mehr als einen Tag unser Angebot genießen wollen, gibt es entweder unseren Zeltplatz, wo auch Ihre Haustiere willkommen sind, oder unsere Luxus-Tipis** – mit Küche und Terrasse, wo Sie mitten in der Natur unter den Sternen ruhig schlafen werden.

* *Erlebnis* – experience

** *Tipi* – teepee

Practice papers Had a go ☐ Nearly there ☐ Nailed it! ☐

Read the following statements and write the correct letters in each box.

Write **A** if only statement A is correct

B if only statement B is correct

A+B if both statements are correct.

19	A	The theme park is in Austria.
	B	The theme park is a new development.

(1 mark)

20	A	The park is not great for children.
	B	The park is great for all age groups.

(1 mark)

21	A	All children must be accompanied by an adult.
	B	Children over 12 can explore the park alone.

(1 mark)

22	A	The water play area is huge.
	B	The water play area is quite new.

(1 mark)

23	A	Hotel accommodation is available at the park.
	B	You can camp at the theme park.

(1 mark)

24	A	The teepees have luxury bathrooms.
	B	The teepees have kitchens.

(1 mark)

Where I live

You read these blogs about where people live.

Alina
Es gibt bestimmt Vorteile, in der Großstadt zu leben, und ich bin glücklich. Die öffentlichen Verkehrsmittel sind relativ billig, und ich kann mit der Straßenbahn schnell zu meinem Arbeitsplatz fahren. Als ich noch weiter entfernt wohnte, war ich gezwungen, jeden Tag mit dem Auto zu fahren, was nicht nur teuer, sondern auch nicht gut für die Umwelt war.

Lukas
Es gefällt mir sehr, dass ich endlich nicht mehr in der Stadt wohne. Ich habe lange darauf gewartet. Letztes Jahr habe ich ein altes Haus in einem Dorf gekauft, wo das Leben viel ruhiger ist. Ich arbeite immer noch, aber jetzt darf ich meine Arbeit meistens zu Hause machen. Ich fahre nur dann ins Büro, wenn es ab und zu ein Geschäftstreffen gibt.

Mohamed
Ich würde nie auf dem Land wohnen. Ich bin in der Stadt geboren und fühle mich hier gut, weil es viele Leute, starken Verkehr, gute Transportmittel und die besten Einkaufsmöglichkeiten gibt. Obwohl die Luft manchmal verschmutzt ist, hat man hier alles was man braucht.

Had a go ☐ **Nearly there** ☐ **Nailed it!** ☐   **Practice papers**

Read the following statements and write the correct letters in each box.

Write **A** if only statement A is correct

B if only statement B is correct

A+B if both statements are correct.

25	A	Alina loves where she now lives.
	B	She misses her morning drive to work.

(1 mark)

26	A	Lukas lives in a modern flat.
	B	He enjoys a quiet life.

(1 mark)

27	A	Lukas can now work from home.
	B	He never needs to go into the office.

(1 mark)

28	A	Mohamed was born in the city.
	B	He appreciates what city life has to offer.

(1 mark)

Being green
You read these comments on social media.

> Meiner Meinung nach hat es heute keinen Sinn mehr, umweltfreundlich zu sein. Unsere Welt ist schon kaputt. Seit Jahren schicken Fabriken schmutziges Gase in die Luft, Tiere verlieren ihren Lebensraum* und es gibt immer mehr Verkehr auf den Straßen und Flugzeuge in der Luft. Unsere Seen sind verschmutzt, es gibt überall Müll … der Mensch zerstört die Natur.
>
> **Noah**
>
> Das Wichtigste ist, dass jeder von uns umweltfreundlich handelt, um diese schlimme Situation zu verbessern. Wir können alle etwas Positives tun, auch wenn es nicht viel ist. Wir sollen daran denken, im Alltag Wasser und Energie zu sparen. Das ist total möglich. Wenn wir einkaufen, sollen wir darauf achten, was wir kaufen – Recyclingprodukte wie Hefte aus Altpapier sind besser. Sie sind **nachhaltig**, denn man kann die Materialien recyceln und wieder benutzen.
>
> **Jana**

* *Lebensraum* – habitat

Complete the sentences in **English**. Write **one** word in each space.

29 Noah thinks it is now …………………… to be environmentally friendly. **(1 mark)**

30 Noah says that factories have …………………… the air for years. **(1 mark)**

31 Noah says that there is …………………… everywhere. **(1 mark)**

32 Jana believes that we could all consume less …………………… . **(1 mark)**

33 Jana says we should be …………………… about what we buy. **(1 mark)**

34 Read the last sentence again. What does **nachhaltig** mean?

Write the correct letter in the box.

A	available
B	organic
C	sustainable

(1 mark)

Practice papers — Had a go ☐ Nearly there ☐ Nailed it! ☐

School life

You read these comments about school life.

> **Max**
> Ich habe ein gutes Jahr in der Schule gehabt. In den meisten Fächern waren meine Noten nicht schlecht, und meine Eltern waren damit zufrieden. Ich habe dieses Jahr versucht, ernster zu sein und mich besser zu konzentrieren, und diese Veränderungen haben Vorteile gebracht. Ich hoffe, dass ich jetzt in die Oberstufe gehen kann, um Abitur zu machen.
>
> **Lea**
> Ich habe mein Schulleben immer schwierig gefunden, weil ich mich nie für den Unterricht interessiert habe. Meine Interessen sind Tanzen und Musik, und ich möchte Schauspielerin werden. Letztes Jahr musste ich sitzenbleiben. Das war so ein Schock, dass ich dieses Jahr hart arbeite, und ich habe angefangen, größere Erfolge zu haben. Die Zukunft sieht positiver aus.

Who do the following statements refer to?

Write **M** for **Max**

L for **Lea**

M+L for **Max** and **Lea.**

35 Who had a good year in school this year? ☐ (1 mark)

36 Who has plans to continue at school? ☐ (1 mark)

37 Who knows what they want to do as a career? ☐ (1 mark)

38 Who has tried hard at school this year? ☐ (1 mark)

SECTION B

Translation into English

39 Translate these sentences into **English**.

Zu Hause essen wir am Abend zusammen und sprechen über den Tag.

.... (2 marks)

Sport gefällt mir sehr, und ich spiele dreimal in der Woche mit meiner Mannschaft.

.... (2 marks)

Wenn es möglich ist, verbringe ich gern Zeit mit meinen Freunden.

.... (2 marks)

Nächstes Jahr hoffe ich, an der Uni Wissenschaft zu studieren.

.... (2 marks)

Ich habe neulich ein tolles Geschenk für meine Stiefmutter im Internet gefunden.

.... (2 marks)

TOTAL FOR PAPER = 50 MARKS

Had a go ☐ Nearly there ☐ Nailed it! ☐   **Practice papers**

Paper 4: Writing (Higher)

In the real exam, you will write your answers on the question paper. Here, you will need to write some of the answers on your own paper.

SECTION A

Translation into German

1 Translate the following sentences into **German**.

I always eat healthy food.

....

He is not interested in celebrities.

....

I hope to have a big party for my birthday this summer.

....

We all understand that it is dangerous to spend too much time online.

....

I met some new friends when I was on holiday.

....

(10 marks)

SECTION B

A letter

2 Choose either Question 2(a) or Question 2(b).

(a) Write a letter to your Swiss friend about your lifestyle. You **must** include the following points: • how you keep fit and healthy • what you ate and drank yesterday • how you will relax this evening.	(b) Write a letter to a German friend about technology. You **must** include the following points: • how you use your mobile phone • what you have done recently on the internet • how you will use social media in the future.

Write your answer in **German**. You should aim to write approximately **90** words.   **(15 marks)**

SECTION C

A post

3 Choose either Question 3(a) or Question 3(b).

(a) Write a post for a German forum for young people about free time. You **must** include the following points: • why free time is important for young people • how you will balance work and free time in the future.	(b) Write an online post about the environment. You **must** include the following points: • why protecting the environment is important • actions you have taken in the past to help the environment.

Write your answer in **German**. You should aim to write approximately **150** words.   **(25 marks)**

TOTAL FOR PAPER = 50 MARKS

Answers

The answers to the Speaking and Writing activities below are sample answers – there are many ways you could answer these questions.

1. Physical descriptions
1. (a) B (b) C (c) A (d) C (e) B
2. Ich bin sechzehn Jahre alt und ziemlich groß.
Ich habe kurze braune Haare.
Mein Freund / Meine Freundin hat ein rundes Gesicht und blaue Augen.
Meine Brüder sind kleiner als ich.
Sie ist schön und sieht sportlich aus.

2. Character descriptions
1. Ich glaube, dass ich normalerweise lustig und positiv bin. Ich kann manchmal faul sein, aber nicht sehr oft. Mein Bruder ist sehr nett und sportlich. Wir machen viel zusammen. Meine beste Freundin heißt Hannah. Sie ist klein und sehr freundlich. Wir gehen oft einkaufen und wir spielen Tennis in dem Park.
2. Reading aloud text and sample answers to follow-on questions: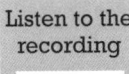
   (a) Ich bin nett, freundlich und meistens zufrieden. Ich habe viele Freunde und ich bin glücklich.
   (b) Meine Schwester ist klein, aber oft böse. Ich finde sie ärgerlich und laut.
   (c) Meine beste Freundin heißt Mia. Sie ist immer nett und lieb und ist sehr lustig.
   (d) Ich gehe zweimal in der Woche mit Freunden aus, normalerweise am Freitagabend und dann am Samstag.

3. My family
1. (a) B (b) B (c) B (d) C
2. Sample answer:
   Auf dem ersten Foto gibt es eine große Familie. Ich sehe neun Personen, sechs Erwachsene und drei Kinder. Ich denke, die Großeltern sind auch da. Der Opa sieht ziemlich alt aus und hat graue Haare.
   Es ist vielleicht eine Party zu Hause. Ein Mädchen hat lange braune Haare.
   Auf dem zweiten Foto sehe ich eine Mutter und ihre Tochter im Park. Vielleicht spielt das Mädchen gern hier. Das Wetter sieht gut aus. Die Mutter hat lange schwarze Haare und braune Augen und trägt eine schwarze Jacke. Die Tochter ist sehr glücklich und hat auch lange dunkle Haare.
   Sample answers to follow-on questions:
   (a) Meine Familie ist nicht sehr groß. Es gibt meine Mutter, meinen Stiefvater, meine Schwester und mich. Wir verstehen uns gut. Meine Mutter ist sehr lieb, mein Stiefvater ist lustig, und meine Schwester und ich sind beide sportlich.
   (b) Gestern habe ich mit Freunden Tennis gespielt. Wir sind in den Park gegangen und haben dort Eis gegessen. Das war toll, weil das Wetter schön war.
   (c) Ich bin nicht sicher, aber ich denke, ich werde nicht heiraten. Ich möchte lieber mit meiner Freundin zusammenleben. Ich weiß nicht, ob wir später Kinder haben werden.

4. Friends
1. Sample answer:
   Ich habe viele Freundinnen und Freunde, aber ein sehr guter Freund von mir heißt Can. Er ist sechzehn Jahre alt. Ich finde, er ist ein guter Freund, weil er immer nett und nie böse ist. Meine Freunde sind wichtig für mich, weil wir immer etwas zusammen machen. Letzten Freitag, bin ich nach der Schule mit meinen Freunden ins Kino gegangen. Wir haben eine tolle Komödie gesehen! Am Samstag werden wir im Park Fußball spielen. Am Sonntag fahren wir mit dem Bus in die Stadt, weil das immer Spaß macht.
2. Sample answers: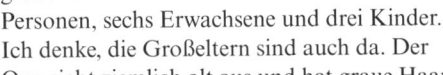
Teacher: Du sprichst mit deiner deutschen Freundin. Ich bin deine Freundin.
Teacher: Guten Tag. Sag mir etwas über deine Freunde und Freundinnen.
Student: Ich habe viele Freunde und Freundinnen. Sie sind alle nett und lustig.
Teacher: Sehr schön.
Student: Wie ist dein bester Freund / deine beste Freundin?
Teacher: Mein bester Freund ist sehr sportlich.
Teacher: Warum sind gute Freunde / Freundinnen wichtig für dich?
Student: Wir machen viel zusammen, und meine Freunde verbessern mein Leben.
Teacher: Ja, das stimmt.
Teacher: Was hast du in letzter Zeit mit Freunden / Freundinnen gemacht?
Student: Wir sind am Samstag ins Kino gegangen und haben gestern Fußball gespielt.
Teacher: Schön.
Teacher: Was wirst du dieses Wochenende machen?
Student: Wir werden im Restaurant essen.
Teacher: Sehr gut.

5. Relationships
1. (a) Not getting on. / Difficult to talk to them.
   (b) They don't want to hear.
   (c) He's their only son. / He's gay.
   (d) He has a boyfriend. / He loves him.
   (e) A better relationship with his parents.
2. I have a lot of nice friends. One of my good friends is very positive and funny. I like him because he always has time for me. We do our homework together every day. Yesterday we played computer games.

6. Dealing with problems
1. Sample answer:
   1. Es gibt zwei Mädchen.
   2. Sie sind im Café.
   3. Sie sprechen und trinken Kaffee.
   4. Sie sind nicht glücklich.
   5. Ein Mädchen hat ein Problem.
2. Sample answer:
   Es gibt ein Paar, eine junge Frau und einen Mann, vielleicht ihr Mann. Sie sehen nicht glücklich aus, und ich denke, sie diskutieren und es gibt einen Streit. Sie sind zu Hause im Wohnzimmer. Die Frau hat schwarze Haare und trägt einen Pullover. Der Mann trägt ein Hemd. Es gibt zwei Personen, vielleicht eine Mutter und ihren Sohn. Die Mutter hat hellbraune Haare und sieht nicht glücklich aus. Der Junge trägt ein weißes T-Shirt und ein blaues Hemd. Ich denke, sie verstehen sich nicht gut, und dass es ein Problem gibt. Der Sohn will nicht zuhören.

Sample answers to follow-on questions:
(a) Ich komme meistens gut mit meinen Freunden aus. Wir machen viel zusammen.
(b) Ich habe mit meiner Freundin Streit gehabt, weil sie immer ausgehen will und ich kein Geld habe. Ich finde das traurig, weil ich sie wirklich liebe.
(c) Wenn es ein Problem in der Schule gibt, würde ich mit den Lehrern sprechen. Sonst spreche ich mit meinem Freund.

7. Daily routine
1 Sample answer:
Montag bis Freitag stehe ich immer früh auf, weil ich natürlich in die Schule gehen muss. Normalerweise stehe ich um sieben Uhr auf, damit ich genug Zeit habe, etwas zu essen.
Zum Frühstück esse ich meistens Brot mit Käse und ich trinke Kaffee. Das schmeckt immer gut und gibt mir Energie für den Tag. Dann sammle ich meine Schulbücher ein und verlasse um halb acht das Haus.
Gestern bin ich zu Fuß zur Schule gegangen. Das mache ich fast jeden Tag, aber nicht, wenn es regnet.
Am Samstagmorgen werde ich lange schlafen!

2 Reading aloud text and sample answers to follow-on questions:
(a) Ich stehe um sieben Uhr auf und ziehe mich an. Ich höre Musik und spreche mit meiner Mutter.
(b) Ich esse gern Brot mit Fleisch oder Käse und ich trinke normalerweise Milch. Am Wochenende esse ich manchmal Eier.
(c) Ich fahre mit dem Bus zur Schule. Im Sommer gehe ich zu Fuß.
(d) Ich komme nach Hause und mache meine Hausaufgaben.

8. Clothing and fashion
1 Sample answer:
1 Es gibt zwei Personen, eine junge Frau und einen Mann.
2 Das Wetter ist schön und warm.
3 Sie sind in der Stadt.
4 Sie gehen spazieren.
5 Die Frau trägt ein weißes Kleid und schwarze Schuhe.

2 1 Ich mag diese Hose am liebsten.
2 In der Schule müssen wir eine Uniform tragen.
3 Diese neuen **Sandalen** sind bequem.
4 Es ist mir wichtig, **modisch** auszusehen.
5 Mein Vater trägt keine Brille.

9. Identity
1 (a) ist (b) Er (c) spielen (d) große (e) mich
2 Sample answer:
Ich bin zufrieden mit meinem Leben, und ich weiß, ich habe Glück, keine großen Probleme zu haben. Meine Familie und Freunde sind mir wichtig – ohne sie würde ich traurig sein. Ich treibe Sport mit Freunden und manchmal hören wir Musik zusammen oder gehen ab und zu ins Kino.
Vor zwei Wochen habe ich meiner Freundin Samira mit dem Einkaufen geholfen. Samiras Mutter ist krank, und die Familie hat kein Auto. Wir sind mit dem Bus zum Supermarkt gefahren und haben alles nach Hause gebracht.
Dieses Wochenende werde ich wahrscheinlich Hausaufgaben machen.

10. When I was younger
1 Reading aloud text and sample answers to follow-on questions: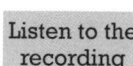
(a) Meine letzte Schule war ziemlich klein. Ich hatte gute Freunde und Freundinnen.
(b) Ich spiele nicht gern Fußball, aber ich mag Tennis und Basketball.
(c) Ich finde meine Lehrer gut. Zwei Lehrer sind zu streng.
(d) Ich gehe gern mit meiner Familie einkaufen oder spazieren.

2 Sample answer:
Auf dem Foto sehe ich sechs Kinder, die ziemlich jung sind. Sie gehen in die Schule. Sie tragen alle eine Schultasche. Das Wetter ist gut.
Es gibt fünf Kinder, die Fußball spielen. Sie sind ziemlich jung.
Sie sind im Park. Es ist Sommer, und sie sehen glücklich aus.
Sample answers to follow-on questions:
(a) Meine letzte Schule war ziemlich klein. Es hat Spaß gemacht.
(b) Als ich jünger war, spielte ich oft Fußball.
(c) Jetzt spiele ich Computerspiele, oder ich gehe mit Freunden ins Kino.

11. My life in the future
1 1 Meine Pläne sind klar.
2 Ich habe Lust, Student zu werden.
3 Ich möchte **Jura** studieren.
4 Dann kann ich später **Anwalt** sein.

2 Sample answer:
In der Woche muss ich natürlich jeden Tag zur Schule gehen. Ich stehe früh auf und esse schnell das Frühstück und verlasse gegen halb acht das Haus. Ich bin den ganzen Tag in der Schule und wenn ich nach Hause komme, muss ich immer Hausaufgaben machen. Ich bin meistens glücklich, aber ich finde den Tag in der Schule zu lang, weil ich immer müde bin. Ich habe aber viele Freundinnen, die sehr lieb sind, und das ist ein positiver Aspekt von meinem Leben. Wir machen viel zusammen, denn wir haben gemeinsame Interessen.
In der Zukunft möchte ich als Journalistin arbeiten und werde zuerst auf der Uni studieren. Ich freue mich sehr darauf. Ich hoffe auch, mehr Freizeit und weniger Stress in meinem Leben zu haben. Ich würde gern mehr Zeit für Sport und Lesen haben. Später will ich heiraten, wenn ich den richtigen Mann finde, aber ich will keine Kinder haben.

12. Food and drink
1 (a) vegetables
(b) cake
(c) coffee
2 (a) C
(b) A
(c) C

13. Meals at home
1 Sample answer:
I don't like / enjoy (eating) vegetables.
In the morning(s) I drink black coffee, which is delicious.
My father cooks the evening meal every day.
Yesterday we ate sausage and / with bread.
When / If I'm hungry, I like eating chips.

2 Reading aloud text and sample answer to follow-on questions:
(a) Ich esse jeden Morgen Brot mit Käse und dann ein Stück Obst. Ich trinke Kaffee.
(b) Ich mag Fastfood, obwohl ich weiß, dass es nicht so gesund ist.
(c) Mein Lieblingsessen ist Fisch mit Pommes. Das kaufen wir am Strand.
(d) Ich esse nicht gern Bananen. Die schmecken mir nicht.

14. Shopping for food

1 Sample answer:
Teacher: Du sprichst mit deiner schweizerischen Freundin. Ich bin deine Freundin.
Teacher: Was isst du gern?
Student: Ich esse gern Fastfood und Curry.
Teacher: Aha.
Teacher: Wie findest du vegetarisches Essen?
Student: Ich mag es nicht, denn ich liebe Fleisch.
Teacher: Alles klar.
Teacher: Wie ist das Essen in der Schule?
Student: Das Essen in der Schule ist nicht schlecht, aber es ist oft kalt.
Teacher: Finde ich auch.
Teacher: Was isst du zu Abend?
Student: Wir essen Fisch und Gemüse.
Teacher: Interessant.
Student: Wo kaufst du Essen?
Teacher: Ich kaufe Essen in dem Supermarkt.

2 Sample answer:
Ich helfe meiner Großmutter / Oma oft beim Einkaufen / mit dem Einkauf.
Es ist nicht einfach für sie, schwere Taschen zu tragen.
Am Samstagmorgen sind wir zum großen Supermarkt in der Stadt gegangen / gefahren.
Nach dem Mittagessen in einem Café haben wir Obst und Gemüse auf dem Markt gekauft.
Wenn ich Zeit habe, werde ich auch das Abendessen kochen.

15. Eating out

1 (a) D (b) E (c) C (d) A
2 (a) P (b) P+N (c) P (d) P (e) N (f) P

16. A healthy diet

1 (a) It stops you feeling hungry.
  (b) They give you energy.
  (c) Occasionally / Every now and then / From time to time
  (d) They make you strong.
  (e) Drink enough water.
  (f) Eating slowly / calmly
  (g) Green foods / vegetables
  (h) Start the day with a good breakfast.

2 Sample answer:
I usually eat healthily, although I sometimes enjoy chips.
They are delicious when you're hungry.
For me, breakfast is the most important meal of the day.
It gives me the energy I need for the whole morning.
Yesterday I ate eggs and bread and tomorrow I'm going to prepare lots of fruit.

17. Sporting events

1 Sample answer:
  1 Auf dem Foto gibt es zwei Mädchen.
  2 Sie spielen Fußball.
  3 Das Wetter ist schön.
  4 Ein Mädchen trägt ein rotes T-Shirt.
  5 Das andere Mädchen trägt ein gelbes T-Shirt und gelbe Schuhe.

2 Sample answer:
Es gibt vier junge Leute, zwei Männer und zwei Frauen. Sie sehen glücklich aus, vielleicht weil das Wetter gut ist. Sie wandern auf dem Land. Sie sind vielleicht im Urlaub. Die Landschaft ist schön, und es gibt viele Bäume. Eine junge Frau trägt ein gelbes T-Shirt, und die andere trägt auch ein T-Shirt.

Auf dem zweiten Foto sehe ich ein Mädchen, das ziemlich jung ist. Sie trägt ein rotes T-Shirt und spielt Tennis. Es gibt auch einen Mann. Er ist vielleicht der Vater des Mädchens oder ihr Trainer. Das ist eine Tennisstunde. Sie sind auf einem Tennisplatz, und das Wetter ist schön. Ich denke, es ist Sommer. Im Hintergrund gibt es große Bäume.

Sample answers to follow-on questions:
(a) Ich mag Wandern, aber ich gehe nicht sehr oft wandern, weil ich in der Stadt wohne. Ich spiele meistens Fußball oder Handball. Ich bin in der Fußballmannschaft in meiner Schule.
(b) Gestern habe ich Handball gespielt, und das hat Spaß gemacht, weil ich mit Freunden gespielt habe. Am Wochenende bin ich schwimmen gegangen.

3 In der Zukunft möchte ich regelmäßig schwimmen gehen, denn Schwimmen ist sehr gut für die Gesundheit. Ich würde auch gern Klettern lernen. Das sieht spannend aus.

18. Advantages of sport

1 I often (do / take) exercise.
I go running every morning.
Sport is really healthy and also a lot of fun.
Yesterday my brother and I played football after school.
When he swims in the sea, he forgets his problems.

2 Reading aloud text and sample answer to follow-on questions:
  (a) Ich denke, der größte Vorteil für mich ist, dass ich besser schlafe und mich positiver fühle.
  (b) Ich gehe jeden Tag laufen und spiele oft Basketball mit meiner Mannschaft. Das macht immer Spaß.
  (c) Letztes Wochenende bin ich schwimmen gegangen und habe eine Wanderung gemacht.
  (d) Heute Abend werde ich Musik hören und ein Buch lesen, bevor ich ins Bett gehe.

19. Physical wellbeing

1 I always sleep well.
My friend and I like playing football.
When / If I have time, I go running in the morning(s).
Last weekend, I went swimming with my stepbrother.
In the future, I would like to play tennis.

2 (a) A+B
  (b) B
  (c) B
  (d) A

20. Mental wellbeing

1 1 Meine Freunde sind mir wichtig.
  2 Ich bewege mich jeden Tag.
  3 Die Prüfungen sind **stressig**.
  4 Es ist entspannend, **Klavier** zu spielen.

2 Sample answers:
Dieses Schuljahr ist sehr wichtig für mich / ist mir sehr wichtig.
Es gibt viel Druck, weil wir im Sommer Prüfungen haben / schreiben.
Wenn ich Fragen habe, spreche ich mit meinem Lehrer / meiner Lehrerin.
Meiner Meinung nach ist es gut, sich zu bewegen und Zeit mit Freunden / Freundinnen zu verbringen.
Man soll immer über seine Probleme sprechen / reden / diskutieren.

21. Feeling unwell

1 Sample answers:
  1 Ich sehe einen Arzt und ein Mädchen.
  2 Das Mädchen trägt ein Hemd und eine Hose.
  3 Der Arzt trägt ein weißes Hemd.
  4 Der Arzt hat graue Haare.
  5 Das Mädchen ist krank und hat Kopfschmerzen.

2 (a) E / B (b) D / C (c) F / H

22. Avoiding health risks
1.
   1. Es gibt fünf junge Menschen.
   2. Sie tanzen und lachen.
   3. Sie sind in einem Klub.
   4. Sie tragen schöne Kleidung.
   5. Ein Mädchen hat blonde Haare.
2. Sample answer:

Ich treibe Sport, um gesund zu sein. Ich mag Fußball und ich bin in der Schulmannschaft für Tennis. Ich bin sehr aktiv.
Meine Gesundheit ist für mich wichtig, deshalb rauche ich nicht. Ich esse auch gesund und ich mag sehr gern Obst, Gemüse und Salat. Ich trinke meistens Wasser.
Letzte Woche bin ich zweimal mit meiner Schwester am Strand laufen gegangen und danach habe ich sehr gut geschlafen. Ein bisschen Ruhe ist auch nötig.
Nach den Prüfungen werde ich mit meinen Freunden eine Party haben. Wir wollen zusammen feiern.

23. My school
1. Sample answers:
   1. Es gibt zwei Schüler in einem Klassenzimmer.
   2. Ich sehe auch einen Lehrer.
   3. Das Mädchen hat lange schwarze Haare.
   4. Der Junge trägt ein T-Shirt.
   5. Sie machen eine Prüfung.
2. Sample answer:

Auf dem ersten Foto gibt es fünf junge Leute, zwei Jungen und drei Mädchen, die Schüler und Schülerinnen sind. Sie kommen aus der Schule und tragen eine Schuluniform, die dunkelrot ist. Sie sind glücklich und sie laufen. Vielleicht ist der Schultag zu Ende. Das Schulgebäude ist im Hintergrund.
Auf dem zweiten Foto sehe ich nochmal fünf Schüler, die in der Schule ankommen. Alle tragen eine Schultasche. Ein Lehrer steht neben der Tür, und ich denke, es ist am Morgen und am Anfang des Tages. Diese Schule ist wahrscheinlich nicht in England, denn die Schüler und Schülerinnen tragen keine Uniform.
Sample answers to follow-on questions:
(a) Ich mag meine Schuluniform und finde es praktisch, dass wir eine bestimmte Kleidung tragen müssen. Obwohl ich die Farbe nicht mag, denke ich, dass eine Uniform eine gute Idee ist.
(b) Gestern haben wir in der Englischstunde über Shakespeare gelernt. Am Nachmittag haben wir Deutsch gelernt.
(c) Ich möchte in der Zukunft Abitur machen und Spanisch, Deutsch und Englisch lernen. Ich werde dann auf die Uni gehen. Ich habe vor, Fremdsprachen zu studieren.

24. School subjects
1. Sample answer:

Teacher: Du sprichst mit deinem österreichischen Freund. Ich bin dein Freund.
Teacher: Was sind deine besten Fächer?
Student: Meine besten Fächer sind Mathe und Physik.
Teacher: Interessant.
Teacher: Wie findest du Hausaufgaben?
Student: Ich weiß, Hausaufgaben sind nötig, aber ich habe oft zu viel zu tun.
Teacher: Ich auch.
Student: Wie findest du deine Schulfächer?
Teacher: Ich finde sie OK.
Teacher: Was möchtest du nächstes Jahr machen?
Student: Ich werde in der Schule bleiben und Abitur machen.
Teacher: Gut.
Teacher: Welches Fach magst du nicht?
Student: Ich mag Englisch nicht. Ich finde es so langweilig.
Teacher: Ich weiß.

2. (a) M (b) J (c) M (d) J (e) R

25. My teachers
1. Sample answer:

Dieses Schuljahr war schwer, weil wir unter Prüfungsdruck waren. Hoffentlich werde ich im Sommer gute Noten bekommen.
Einige Lehrer haben mir geholfen, und ich finde die meisten Lehrer und Lehrerinnen gut, obwohl nicht alle fantastisch sind. Meine Deutschlehrerin ist meine Lieblingslehrerin, weil sie nicht so streng ist. Wir wissen, dass sie das Beste für uns will, und deshalb ist sie sehr beliebt. Andere Lehrer sind nicht so gut, weil sie manchmal böse sind und keine Zeit für uns haben. Unser Mathelehrer kommt spät in die Stunde und ist nicht gut organisiert.
In der Zukunft möchte ich bestimmt nicht Lehrer werden. Ich denke, diese Arbeit ist zu schwer, mit langen Arbeitszeiten. Obwohl man auch lange Ferien hat, muss man als Lehrer jeden Abend, jedes Wochenende und auch in den Ferien arbeiten. Das möchte ich nicht tun. Das Gehalt ist auch nicht gut. Ich würde lieber einen Job mit Technologie haben.

2. Reading aloud text and sample answer to follow-on questions:
   (a) Ich finde meine Lehrer meistens gut und freundlich.
   (b) Ein guter Lehrer versteht die Schüler und kann gut erklären.
   (c) Es ist interessant, wenn man mit jungen Leuten arbeitet, und man hat auch sehr lange Sommerferien.
   (d) Ich will in der Zukunft Fußballspielerin werden. Dann kann ich viel Geld verdienen.

26. The school day
1. Sample answer:

Ich finde den Schultag zu lang und ich denke, der Tag beginnt zu früh, weil ich mehr schlafen möchte. Wir haben sechs Stunden pro Tag, vier am Morgen und zwei am Nachmittag, und die Mittagspause ist um 13:00 Uhr.
Gestern in der Pause habe ich mit meinen Freundinnen gesprochen und habe Kuchen gegessen. Manchmal haben wir Zeit, Fußball zu spielen, aber gestern hat es geregnet und wir haben nicht gespielt.
Morgen werde ich sechs Stunden haben. In der ersten Stunde werde ich Wissenschaft lernen und in der letzten Stunde habe ich Musik.

2. (a) He has his favourite subjects.
   (b) sport
   (c) English and history
   (d) after break
   (e) Maths

27. School uniform
1. Sample answer:

Wenn ich in der Schule bin, muss ich eine Uniform tragen. Ich trage ein blaues Hemd und eine grüne Jacke. Man darf nur schwarze Schuhe tragen, und Sportschuhe sind total verboten. Auf der einen Seite kann die Uniform praktisch sein, denn man muss nicht jeden Morgen nachdenken, welche Kleidung man tragen soll. Auf der anderen Seite mag ich es nicht, dass wir alle dieselbe Kleidung tragen.
Gestern habe ich Fußball gespielt und ich habe schwarze Shorts getragen. Das sieht nicht schön aus, aber ist bequem.
Heute Abend werde ich wie immer eine Hose und ein T-Shirt tragen.

2. Sample answers:

Ich mag die Uniform nicht.
In der Schule tragen wir eine blaue Jacke und ein weißes Hemd.
Die Jungen müssen eine graue Hose tragen.
Man darf nur schwarze Schuhe tragen.
Gestern habe ich rote Socken gekauft. / Gestern kaufte ich rote Socken.

28. School rules

1   Sample answer:
Teacher: Du sprichst mit deinem deutschen Freund. Ich bin dein Freund.
Teacher: Wie findest du die Schulregeln?
Student: Ich finde die Schulregeln normal.
Teacher: Interessant.
Teacher: Welche Regel findest du gut?
Student: Es ist gut, dass Rauchen verboten ist.
Teacher: Ja, klar.
Student: Wie sind die Regeln in deiner Schule?
Teacher: Nicht schlecht.
Teacher: Wie findest du die Schuluniform?
Student: Die Schuluniform ist nicht schön.
Teacher: Ich verstehe.
Teacher: Welche Regel magst du nicht?
Student: Handys sind verboten. Das ist blöd.
Teacher: Ja. Das stimmt.

2   Sample answer:
Teacher: Du sprichst mit deinem österreichischen Freund. Ich bin dein Freund.
Teacher: Warum sind Schulregeln wichtig?
Student: Schulregeln sind wichtig, denn sie machen die Schule sicherer.
Teacher: Interessant.
Teacher: Welche Regel ist die wichtigste?
Student: Ich denke, es ist wichtig, dass Rauchen in der Schule verboten ist, weil Rauchen so ungesund ist.
Teacher: Ja, klar.
Student: Wie sind die Regeln in deiner Schule?
Teacher: Ich finde sie praktisch.
Teacher: Welche Regel findest du nicht gut?
Student: Ich finde es schlecht, dass wir in der Pause in der Schule bleiben müssen. Ich möchte ausgehen und Essen kaufen.
Teacher: Ich verstehe.
Teacher: Was ist die Regel für Handys in der Schule?
Student: Handys sind im Unterricht verboten. Ich denke, das ist eine gute Idee.
Teacher: Das stimmt.

29. Homework

1   Sample answer:
Ich weiß, dass Hausaufgaben wichtig sind, weil man besser lernt, wenn man übt. Es ist auch nicht möglich, alles in der Unterrichtsstunde zu machen. Wir arbeiten aber oft zu viel, und das ist nicht gesund.
Ich verbringe zwei Stunden jeden Abend mit Hausaufgaben. Ich finde das langweilig. Dieses Jahr habe ich Prüfungen und ich muss viel lernen.
Gestern Abend habe ich nur Deutsch gelesen und habe für diese Prüfung gelernt.
Heute Abend werde ich Mathe lernen, weil ich morgen eine Matheprüfung habe. Dieses Fach finde ich schwierig.

2   Sample answer:
In der Schule arbeite ich hart und ich versuche immer, gute Noten zu bekommen / kriegen.
Ich mache jeden Tag viele Hausaufgaben.
Ich denke, dass es wichtig ist, die Verantwortung für sein eigenes Lernen zu übernehmen / akzeptieren.
Gestern Abend habe ich drei Stunden mit Deutschhausaufgaben verbracht.
Das war schwer / schwierig, aber ich glaube, ich verstehe jetzt besser / dass ich jetzt besser verstehe.

30. Stress at school

1   Sample answers:
   (a) Safe / supportive (surroundings)
   (b) Maintain close contact. / Keep talking.
   (c) (Any two): Enough sleep / Regular mealtimes / Homework schedule

2   Reading aloud text and sample answer to follow-on questions:
   (a) Ich finde die Schule sehr schwer. Es gibt zu viel zu tun.
   (b) Ich spreche mit Freunden oder mit meinen Lehrern.
   (c) Ich werde heute Abend für die nächste Prüfung lernen. Sie ist in Geschichte.
   (d) Ich möchte eine Party mit meinen Freunden und Freundinnen haben. Wir werden feiern.

31. My ideal school

1   Sample answers:
   1 Es gibt acht Jungen und Mädchen.
   2 Sie sind ziemlich jung.
   3 Sie kommen aus der Schule.
   4 Das Gebäude ist modern und weiß.
   5 Das Wetter ist gut.

2   1 Alle Schüler finden das Gebäude hässlich.
   2 Die Lehrer sind aber **hervorragend** und kümmern sich um uns.
   3 Wir sollen weniger Hausaufgaben bekommen.
   4 Das wäre ein echter Traum.
   5 Die **Heizung** funktioniert nicht.

32. Preparing for exams

1   Sample answer:
Teacher: Du sprichst mit deiner deutschen Freundin. Ich bin deine Freundin.
Teacher: Wie lange verbringst du jeden Abend mit Schularbeit?
Student: Ich arbeite zwei Stunden jeden Abend.
Teacher: Sehr gut.
Teacher: Und wo arbeitest du?
Student: Ich arbeite in meinem Schlafzimmer.
Teacher: Interessant.
Teacher: Wie oft machst du eine Pause?
Student: Ich mache jede Stunde eine Pause.
Teacher: Gute Idee.
Teacher: Warum arbeitest du so hart?
Student: Ich möchte gute Noten bekommen.
Teacher: Gut.
Student: Wie findest du Prüfungen?
Teacher: Ich finde Prüfungen schwierig.

2   1 Man kann nicht alles in der letzten Minute wiederholen.
   2 Ich habe **Nachhilfestunden** in Biologie.
   3 Ich arbeite drei Stunden täglich.
   4 Während ich lerne, höre ich Musik.
   5 Ich will später **Jura** studieren.

33. Gap year

1   Today I have my last exam.
My brother is travelling through France by train.
Next year, I am going to work with sick animals.
Abroad it is useful to speak other languages.
Some friends want to travel to Europe in the autumn.

2   Sample answers:
   (a) Ich will nächstes Jahr in die Oberstufe gehen, um Kunst, English und Mathe zu lernen. Dann werde ich die Schule verlassen.
   (b) Ich möchte nicht direkt auf die Uni gehen, sondern will ein Jahr reisen, bevor ich ein Studium mache.
   (c) Ich werde vielleicht nach Afrika reisen und in einer Schule für kleine Kinder helfen.
   (d) In der Zukunft möchte ich Mathelehrer werden und in einer Großstadt arbeiten.

(e) Ja, ich habe letztes Jahr als Kellner in einem Café gearbeitet, um Geld zu verdienen. Ich spare das Geld, damit ich in der Zukunft reisen kann.
(f) Freiwillige Arbeit ist eine wunderbare Idee, weil so viele Leute arm sind und Hilfe brauchen.
(g) Ich fahre gern ins Ausland, aber ich denke, ich würde lieber in England arbeiten und leben. Meine Familie ist mir sehr wichtig.
(h) Ich esse sehr gesund, um fit zu bleiben. Sport ist mir wichtig und ich spiele in zwei Mannschaften. Ich trainiere jeden Tag und brauche viel Energie. Ich trinke Wasser, esse Obst und Gemüse und würde nie rauchen, weil es so schlecht für den Körper ist.
(i) Sport macht Spaß, weil man oft mit Freunden und Freundinnen zusammen ist. Es ist die beste Weise, sich regelmäßig zu bewegen. Sport hilft mir, Stress und andere Probleme zu vergessen.
(j) Ich komme sehr gut mit meiner Mutter und mit meinem Bruder aus. Mit meinem Vater ist es nicht so einfach, weil ich ihn nicht so oft sehe. Meine Freunde und ich verstehen uns gut, und es gibt selten Streit.

34. Plans for next year
1   (a) lernen
    (b) Die
    (c) Nächstes
    (d) wird
    (e) bekommen
2   Sample answer:
Teacher: Du sprichst mit deinem deutschen Freund. Ich bin dein Freund.
Teacher: Was möchtest du in der Oberstufe lernen?
Student: Ich möchte Mathe und Wissenschaft lernen. Diese Fächer interessieren mich.
Teacher: Interessant.
Student: Willst du in der Schule bleiben?
Teacher: Ja, bestimmt.
Teacher: Was ist dein bestes Fach dieses Jahr?
Student: Mein bestes Fach ist Mathe. Ich finde es nicht schwer, und meine Noten sind gut.
Teacher: Schön.
Teacher: Möchtest du auf die Uni gehen?
Student: Ja, ich möchte Wissenschaft studieren.
Teacher: Gut.
Teacher: Was für eine Arbeit möchtest du in der Zukunft haben?
Student: Ich will bei einer Bank arbeiten.
Teacher: Gute Idee.

35. Future studies
1   Sample answers:
    1 Es gibt sechs Jugendliche.
    2 Sie sind wahrscheinlich Schüler oder Studenten.
    3 Sie sitzen in einem Park und sprechen.
    4 Es gibt drei Jungen und drei Mädchen.
    5 Im Hintergrund gibt es ein modernes Gebäude.
2   Sample answer:
Auf dem ersten Foto sehe ich ein großes modernes Gebäude. Ich denke, das ist eine Uni, denn es gibt viele Studenten und Studentinnen. Vorne sind drei junge Leute, zwei junge Frauen und ein junger Mann. Sie haben Bücher mit.
Auf dem zweiten Foto gibt es nochmal fünf Studenten und Studentinnen. Sie machen eine Pause und sitzen zusammen in einem Garten an der Uni. Sie sprechen miteinander. Ein Mädchen auf der rechten Seite hat lange dunkle Haare und trägt ein T-Shirt.

Sample answers to follow-on questions:
(a) Ich möchte gern auf die Uni gehen. Ich will Englisch studieren.
(b) Es ist toll, sein bestes Fach weiter zu studieren und dann bessere Arbeitsmöglichkeiten zu haben. Man findet auch viele neue Freunde oder Freundinnen, aber ein Studium kostet viel Geld. Das ist ein großer Nachteil.
(c) Ich plane, zuerst ins Ausland zu reisen, um freiwillig zu arbeiten, und dann ein Studium zu machen. Danach werde ich eine Arbeitsstelle suchen.

36. Future career
1   Sample answer:
Es ist wichtig für mich, mit vielen Leuten zu arbeiten und nicht allein in einem kleinen Büro. Ich bin nicht gern allein und mag es, in einem Team zu arbeiten. Lustige Mitarbeiter machen das Leben besser. Geld ist nicht alles, aber ich möchte genug verdienen. Dann kann ich unabhängig sein, eine Wohnung finden und nicht mehr zu Hause wohnen.
Ich habe im Sommer in einem Kleidungsgeschäft gearbeitet. Es war toll, aber ich war immer müde.
In der Zukunft werde ich an der Uni studieren. Dann will ich in einer Schule mit kleinen Kindern arbeiten.
2   Reading aloud text and sample answer to follow-on questions:
(a) Ich will in der Zukunft Lehrer werden. Ich möchte Fremdsprachen unterrichten und mit Jugendlichen arbeiten.

(b) Ich will auf die Uni gehen. Ich denke, das wird eine tolle Erfahrung sein, obwohl es wirklich zu teuer ist.
(c) Ich habe keine Lust, reich zu sein, aber ich will genug verdienen, damit ich ein gutes Leben haben kann – und ich will gut essen, ein Auto haben und ausgehen.
(d) Ich möchte gern freiwillig im Ausland arbeiten, bevor ich auf die Uni gehe.

37. Opinions about jobs
1   Sample answer:
Ich denke, es ist wichtig, dass man gut bezahlt wird, sonst wird man unglücklich, besonders wenn die Arbeit schwer ist. Freundliche Mitarbeiter und Mitarbeiterinnen sind meiner Meinung nach auch etwas Positives, weil man dann glücklicher ist. Ich würde auch gern in einem modernen Gebäude arbeiten, wo es hell ist und es große Fenster gibt.
Ich habe bis jetzt keinen Job gehabt, weil es leider in meiner Stadt nicht viele Jobs für Jugendliche gibt. Ich hoffe, ich werde diesen Sommer in einem Schuhgeschäft arbeiten, denn sie brauchen eine Verkäuferin.
In der Zukunft will ich im Bereich Informatik arbeiten.
2   I like art and English.
In my free time I like reading.
In the future, I would like somehow to work with books.
It is important for me to enjoy my working day.
I hope that I will find the right job with nice colleagues / co-workers.

38. Free-time activities
1   Sample answer:
Ich sehe sechs Personen, vier Männer und zwei junge Frauen. Sie sind in einem Kunstmuseum und sehen sich die Bilder an. Ein Mann spricht über ein Bild.
Es gibt sechs junge Leute, vier Mädchen und zwei Jungen. Sie sind glücklich. Sie sind am Strand, vielleicht im Urlaub. Es ist Sommer, und das Wetter ist schön.

Sample responses to follow-up questions:
(a) Ich mag Kunst in der Schule, denn es ist einfach.
(b) Ich gehe gern ins Kino und ich spiele Fußball.
(c) Ich habe Fußball im Park gespielt. Dann habe ich mit Freunden im Café gegessen.

2 (a) working in the garden / gardening
   (b) 26%
   (c) going to the gym
   (d) B

39. Music and dance
1 Sample answer:
Auf dem ersten Foto gibt es eine Band. Es gibt zwei Männer und zwei junge Frauen, die Musik machen. Drei Personen spielen Instrumente, und die Sängerin sieht toll aus. Sie hat dunkle Haare und trägt eine schwarze Hose. Sie sind vielleicht in einem Club.
Auf dem zweiten Foto gibt es drei Freundinnen. Sie sind in einem Club. Sie tanzen und sehen glücklich aus. Zwei Mädchen haben braune Haare, und das andere Mädchen trägt ein schönes Kleid. Sie tragen coole Partykleidung.
Sample answers to follow-on questions:
(a) Ich mag Live-Musik. Ich gehe manchmal zu einem Konzert.
(b) Ich höre gern Metal und Rapmusik, aber ich mag Pop nicht.
(c) Ich habe letztes Jahr ein Konzert von King Creosote gesehen, das fantastisch war. Er ist ein Sänger aus Schottland und hat eine sehr gute Band. Es war ein toller Abend.
2 (a) A   (b) C   (c) A   (d) B

40. Arranging to go out
1 (a) B
   (b) A
   (c) C
   (d) A
   (e) B
2 1 Ich habe einen netten neuen Freund.
   2 Wir haben uns auf der Kegelbahn kennengelernt.
   3 Wir gehen oft zusammen aus.
   4 Zum Geburtstag hat er mir Sekt gekauft.
   5 Nächste Woche wollen wir wandern.

41. Reading
1 Sample answer:
Obwohl ich gern lese, lese ich nicht sehr oft, denn ich habe nicht viel Freizeit. Dieses Jahr gibt es einfach zu viel zu lernen. In den Ferien und manchmal am Abend finde ich noch ein bisschen Zeit, ein Buch zu genießen.
Ich mag besonders Liebesgeschichten für Jugendliche und habe vor kurzem den Roman „Heartstopper" von Alice Oseman gelesen. Das ist eine tolle Geschichte, obwohl sie manchmal traurig ist. Wenn ich nach den Prüfungen Freizeit habe, werde ich den neuen Roman von Alice Oseman lesen. Ich möchte auch einige Krimis lesen, weil sie spannender als Liebesgeschichten sind.
2 Sample answers:
Ich lese gern / mag Lesen und habe immer ein Buch mit.
Als ich jünger war, habe ich alle die ganzen Harry Potter Bücher gelesen.
Jetzt lese ich lieber Krimis.
Zurzeit / Im Moment lese ich einen neuen Roman, der „Die Regeln" heißt.
Die Hauptperson ist ein Junge, der Computer liebt.

42. Television
1 Reading aloud text and sample answer to follow-on questions:
   (a) Ich sehe gern Spielshows und ich mag auch Krimis.
   (b) Ich sehe gern Tennis im Fernsehen, aber Fußball finde ich laut und langweilig.
   (c) Ich denke, Filme sind besser im Kino, denn so ist es spannender.
   (d) Ich mag „The Simpsons". Mein Bruder und ich sehen jeden Tag diese Sendung und finden sie sehr lustig.

2 Sample answer:
Teacher: Du sprichst mit deinem deutschen Freund. Ich bin dein Freund.
Teacher: Wie oft siehst du fern?
Student: Ich sehe einmal oder zweimal pro Woche fern.
Teacher: Interessant.
Teacher: Und was für Sendungen siehst du gern?
Student: Ich mag Krimis und auch Sportsendungen.
Teacher: Alles klar.
Student: Siehst du gern fern?
Teacher: Nein … ich sehe lieber Filme online.
Student: Wie findest du Gewalt im Fernsehen?
Teacher: Ich finde es schrecklich. Es ist sehr schlimm für Jugendliche, Gewalt zu sehen.
Student: Das stimmt.
Teacher: Welche Sendungen interessieren Jugendliche?
Student: Ich denke, Jugendliche lieben Filme, Krimiserien und Sportsendungen – und auch lustige Komödien.
Teacher: Interessant.

43. Film and cinema
1 (a) finde   (d) spannende
   (b) den   (e) Der
   (c) gibt
2 Sample answers:
I rarely go to the cinema because the tickets are so expensive nowadays.
But I think it's a good experience when I see a film with friends.
In my opinion, the best films are action films and war films.
Everything happens very fast and it's always exciting.
Last month, I saw a German detective film / thriller.

44. Celebrations
1 Sample answers:
   1 Es gibt sechs junge Leute, zwei Männer und vier Frauen.
   2 Eine Frau hat Geburtstag.
   3 Es gibt einen großen Kuchen.
   4 Sie trinken und lachen.
   5 Die Party macht Spaß.
2 In meiner Familie feiern wir jeden Geburtstag.
   Wir machen das, um mehr Zeit zusammen zu verbringen und Spaß zu haben.
   Mein älterer Bruder hat im April Geburtstag.
   Letztes Jahr sind wir für das Wochenende nach Frankreich gefahren.
   Nächstes Jahr möchte ich eine große Party zu Hause / bei mir haben.

45. Customs and festivals
1 (a) F
   (b) P
2 Sample answer:
Teacher: Du sprichst mit deiner schweizerischen Freundin. Ich bin deine Freundin.
Teacher: Was machst du normalerweise an Weihnachten?
Student: Wir essen mit der Familie zu Hause.
Teacher: Sehr gut.
Teacher: Und wie findest du Familienfeste?
Student: Feste mit meiner Familie machen viel Spaß.
Teacher: Interessant.
Teacher: Wie feierst du deinen Geburtstag?
Student: Ich gehe mit Freunden aus.
Teacher: Schön.
Teacher: Was ist dein Lieblingsgeburtstagsgeschenk?
Student: Ich mag Kleidung oder Geld oder ein neues Handy.
Teacher: Gut.
Student: Wie findest du Feste?
Teacher: Ich denke, sie sind lustig.

46. Places of interest
1 Sample answers:
   1 Es gibt vier junge Leute, zwei Mädchen und zwei Jungen.
   2 Sie sind vielleicht Freunde.
   3 Ein Junge trägt rote Schuhe und eine Hose.
   4 Sie sind in London im Urlaub.
   5 Sie gehen über eine Brücke und lachen.
2 Sample answer:
Ich wohne in der Nähe von York. Mein Dorf hat nicht viel Interessantes. Nicht weit von uns gibt es ein bekanntes Museum, das Bahnmuseum, wo man viele alte und moderne Züge sehen kann.
Auch in York kann man historische Gebäude und die alte Stadtmauer sehen oder auf dem Markt einkaufen gehen. Letztes Jahr bin ich nach Durham gefahren. Das ist eine schöne alte Stadt mit viel Geschichte. Das Schloss hat uns sehr gefallen, weil es so groß war.
In der Zukunft möchte ich nach Cambridge fahren, um die berühmte Universität zu besuchen.

47. Traditions
1 (a) sixteen / 16
   (b) autumn
   (c) experience
   (d) popular
   (e) tents
   (f) C
2 Sample answers:
   1 Ich sehe elf Leute, Männer und Frauen.
   2 Sie sind auf dem Weihnachtsmarkt.
   3 Sie kaufen Geschenke.
   4 Es ist Winter und sehr kalt.
   5 Es gibt Schnee.

48. Learning languages
1 Reading aloud text and sample answer to follow-on questions: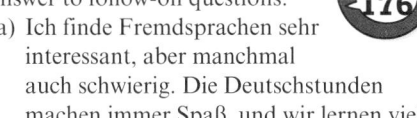
   (a) Ich finde Fremdsprachen sehr interessant, aber manchmal auch schwierig. Die Deutschstunden machen immer Spaß, und wir lernen viel.
   (b) Mit Sprachkenntnissen ist es einfach zu reisen und mit anderen Menschen zu sprechen. Man kann auch die Kultur besser verstehen.
   (c) Nach dem Abitur werde ich auf die Uni gehen. Ich werde Mathe und Deutsch studieren. Ich möchte in Deutschland arbeiten.
   (d) Man kann ein anderes Land und andere Leute kennenlernen, und man hat bessere Arbeitsmöglichkeiten.
2 (a) P+N
   (b) P
   (c) N
   (d) (i) She has great / fun teachers.
       (ii) They make lessons exciting.

49. Celebrity culture
1 (a) B
   (b) N
   (c) N
   (d) A
   (e) B
2 Sample answer: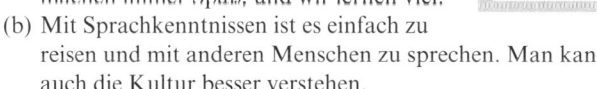
Teacher: Du sprichst mit deiner deutschen Freundin. Ich bin deine Freundin.
Teacher: Welchen Star magst du?
Student: Ich mag den Sänger Pacca Pacciere.
Teacher: Schön.
Student: Hast du einen Lieblingsstar?
Teacher: Ja … sie ist eine Fußballspielerin.
Teacher: Glaubst du, dass Stars wichtig sind?
Student: Nein … nicht wirklich. Sie sind interessant und dann verschwinden sie.
Teacher: Stimmt.
Teacher: Was hat dein Lieblingsstar in letzter Zeit gemacht?
Student: Er hat in London ein kostenloses Konzert gegeben.
Teacher: Fantastisch.
Teacher: Was wirst du heute Abend im Internet ansehen?
Student: Ich werde Paccas Musik herunterladen und Videos ansehen.
Teacher: Gute Idee.

50. Opinions about being a celebrity
1 Sample answers:
   1 Ich sehe eine junge Frau, einen Star.
   2 Sie ist schön und hat blonde Haare.
   3 Es gibt viele Journalisten.
   4 Sie machen Fotos.
   5 Die Frau ist traurig.
2 Reading aloud text and sample answer to follow-on questions:
   (a) Mein Lieblingsstar ist ein britischer Schauspieler. Er ist schön und sehr bekannt.
   (b) Man ist reich und kann alles kaufen, was man will. Man hat auch viele Fans.
   (c) Ja. Weil Journalisten immer da sind, kann man kein Privatleben haben. Das finde ich sehr schlimm.
   (d) Ich folge einigen Bands, denn ich liebe ihre Musik, und ich folge auch einigen Künstlern.

51. Sports stars
1 (a) B
   (b) A
   (c) A
   (d) B
2 Sample answer:
Auf dem Foto sehe ich einen Mann, der Tennis spielt. Er ist in einem Stadion. Es ist Nacht, aber die Lichter sind hell. Der Mann trägt weiße Tenniskleidung. Er wirft den Ball in die Luft und wird ihn schlagen.
Auf dem zweiten Foto gibt es zwei Frauen, die Fußball spielen. Sie sind draußen auf einem Fußballplatz, und das Wetter ist nicht schlecht. Es gibt Bäume im Hintergrund. Eine Frau trägt ein blaues T-Shirt, und die andere trägt ein weißes T-Shirt. Beide Frauen haben lange dunkle Haare. Der Ball ist weiß.
Sample answers to follow-up questions:
(a) Ich liebe Andy Murray. Er war ein toller Tennisstar und war sehr erfolgreich. Ich mag Tennis und ich spiele oft im Sommer. Ich mag es, draußen zu spielen.
(b) Letztes Wochenende bin ich mit meinen Freunden schwimmen gegangen. Das war schön, aber ich war danach sehr müde.
(c) In der Zukunft würde ich am liebsten Tauchen ausprobieren. Das sieht spannend aus.

52. Celebrity events
1 Sample answer:
Teacher: Du sprichst mit deinem deutschen Freund. Ich bin dein Freund.
Teacher: Wer ist dein Lieblingsstar?
Student: Mein Lieblingsstar ist Beyoncé.
Teacher: Schön.
Teacher: Was ist ein negativer Aspekt, wenn man berühmt ist?
Student: Ich denke, man hat kein Privatleben.
Teacher: Interessant.
Student: Welchen Star magst du?
Teacher: Ich mag den Sänger Bruce Springsteen.
Teacher: Welches Live-Konzert hast du gesehen?
Student: Ich habe ein Nickelback-Konzert in London gesehen.

Teacher: Fantastisch.
Teacher: Welche Band möchtest du in der Zukunft sehen?
Student: Ich möchte Maruja sehen, weil ich diese Musik liebe.
Teacher: Gute Idee.

2 Sample answers:
Mein Lieblingsstar ist ein Fußballer / Fußballspieler / Fußballerin / Fußballspielerin.
Am Samstag / Samstags gehe ich oft zum Spiel.
Mein Bruder hört immer Musik.
Wir laden Videos aus dem Internet herunter.
Letztes Jahr habe ich ein tolles Konzert in dem Park gesehen / sah ich ein tolles Konzert im Park.

53. Celebrities for the environment
1   (a) B
    (b) A
    (c) A+B
2   (a) (initiative for) green energy
    (b) electricity direct from the sun / 1,900 solar panels providing (over) 70% of the energy (they use)
    (c) collecting rainwater / using rainwater

54. Holiday activities
1 Sample answer:
Ich fahre nach Marbella in Spanien.
Wir fliegen von Manchester nach Marbella. Das ist sehr schnell.
Das Wetter ist warm, und die Sonne scheint jeden Tag.
Wir gehen zum Strand. Es ist schön, denn das Meer ist blau und wir gehen schwimmen.
Das Essen ist toll. Ich esse Fisch mit Pommes.
2 (a) mountains
    (b) beach
    (c) America

55. Holiday accommodation
1 1 Er fährt jedes Jahr nach Spanien.
    2 Wir besuchen die Familie.
    3 Meine Tante hat einen **Wohnwagen**.
    4 Das Hotel war total **ausgebucht**.
2 Reading aloud text and sample answer to follow-on questions:

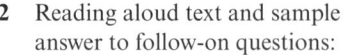

(a) Ich verbringe gern Zeit mit Freunden, wenn ich keine Schule habe. Das macht immer Spaß.
(b) Letztes Jahr habe ich im Sommer einen Kunstkurs gemacht.
(c) Ich sehe jeden Tag meine Freunde und Freundinnen. Wir treiben Sport, machen Ausflüge und gehen in die Stadt oder ins Kino.
(d) Mein idealer Urlaub wäre ein aktiver Urlaub in den Bergen. Ich möchte in die Schweiz fahren, um die schöne Landschaft zu sehen und um Deutsch zu sprechen.

56. Other holiday accommodation
1 Reading aloud text and sample answer to follow-on questions:

(a) Ich fahre manchmal nach London oder nach Cornwall. Das ist schön.
(b) Ich mag Reisen, aber es ist teuer. Fliegen ist fantastisch und sehr schnell.
(c) Ich finde es besser, mit meiner Familie zu fahren. Alles ist gut organisiert.
(d) Im Sommer will ich nach Edinburgh fahren. Ich will das Festival sehen.

2 Reading aloud text and sample answer to follow-on questions:
(a) In meiner Gegend gibt es einen schönen Wald und ein altes Kunstmuseum. Man kann wandern gehen.

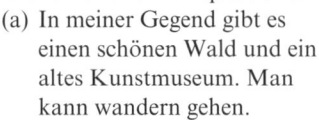

(b) Ich bin letztes Jahr nach London gefahren und habe ein Fußballspiel gesehen. Das hat Spaß gemacht.
(c) Dieses Jahr fahre ich mit Freunden nach Spanien, um das Ende der Prüfungen zu feiern.
(d) Ich mag einen Urlaub am Strand, wenn es warm ist, weil man im Meer schwimmen kann.

57. Opinions about travelling
1 Sample answer:
Auf dem ersten Foto sehe ich ein Mädchen und einen Jungen, die mit dem Bus fahren. Sie sehen glücklich und entspannt aus und lächeln. Das Mädchen trägt ein graues T-Shirt und hat braune mittellange Haare, und ihr Freund trägt ein Hemd.

Sie fahren vielleicht in die Stadt. Es gibt viele andere Leute im Bus.
Auf dem zweiten Foto sehe ich ein Flugzeug. Im Flugzeug sitzen vier Personen. Ein Mann sitzt neben einem Fenster. Dieser Mann und eine Frau trinken Kaffee und sie lächeln beide.
Sample answers to follow-on questions:
(a) Ich fahre jeden Tag mit dem Bus zur Schule. Das ist praktisch und ziemlich schnell. Oft gibt es aber zu viele Leute, und ich muss den ganzen Weg nach Hause stehen, was nicht so bequem ist.
(b) Ich bin letztes Jahr nach Amerika geflogen. Meine Familie und ich haben zwei Wochen bei meinem Onkel in Kalifornien verbracht. Der Flug war lang, aber es war ein wunderbarer Urlaub.
(c) Meine Traumreise wäre nach Australien. Ich habe so viel über das Land gelesen und möchte es gerne richtig entdecken.
2 Sample answer:
Meine Mutter hat ein Auto, aber ich kann nicht fahren. Das Auto ist praktisch.
Ich fahre mit dem Fahrrad, wenn es warm ist.
Ich fahre mit dem Bus zur Schule. Das ist nicht bequem, aber ich bin mit meinen Freundinnen.
Ich fahre nie mit dem Zug, denn es ist teuer.
Fliegen ist toll und sehr schnell.

58. Planning a future holiday
1 Sample answer:
Als ich ein Kind war, haben wir die Sommerferien im Ausland verbracht, wo das Wetter wärmer ist und man in der Sonne liegen oder im Meer schwimmen kann. Jetzt haben wir nicht so viel Geld, und ein Urlaub im Ausland ist zu teuer. Manchmal bleiben wir im Sommer zu Hause.
Vor einigen Jahren sind wir nach Berlin gefahren. Die Großstadt war wunderschön, und es gab so viel zu sehen. Ich habe mein Deutsch geübt, obwohl viele Leute Englisch sprechen.
Diesen Sommer werde ich einen Job finden und mein eigenes Geld verdienen, weil ich ein Auto kaufen will und Geld sparen muss.
2 (a) C
    (b) D
    (c) E

59. Past holidays
1 Das Hotel war bequem und modern.
Es gab einen schönen Strand.
Die Leute waren sehr freundlich.
Ich habe Geschenke für meine Freunde und Familie gekauft.
Das Wetter war gut, und es war jeden Tag warm.

2   Letztes Jahr sind wir nach Österreich in den Urlaub gefahren.
    Meine Großeltern wohnen dort in den Bergen, also brauchen wir kein Hotel.
    Wir sind eine Woche geblieben, und das Wetter war die ganze Zeit gut.
    Ich bin in dem See schwimmen gegangen.
    Am letzten Tag haben wir ein traditionelles Mittagessen gegessen.

60. Holiday problems
1   Sample answer:
Letzten Sommer waren wir zwei Wochen in Deutschland. Wir haben in einem kleinen Ferienhaus auf dem Land gewohnt. Das Wetter war meistens gut, und wir haben die Landschaft schön gefunden.
Das Haus war leider zu klein für unsere Familie und es gab nicht genug Platz. Das war ärgerlich, weil das Ferienhaus gar nicht billig war. Das Badezimmer und die Küche waren ein bisschen schmutzig. Es gab auch keinen Garten und nicht genug heißes Wasser.
Nächstes Jahr will ich nach Spanien fahren. Ich werde in einem Hotel wohnen und ein tolles Badezimmer haben.
2   1 Letztes Jahr war ich in den Bergen in Österreich.
    2 Die **Unterkunft** in einer **Hütte** war schmutzig.
    3 Die Zugreise hat lange gedauert.
    4 Das Wetter war schlecht.
    5 Das Frühstück hat nicht geschmeckt.

61. Making a complaint
1   (a) essen
    (b) die
    (c) bestellt
    (d) Mein
    (e) kein
2   Sample answer:
Ich hatte am Freitag letzter Woche Geburtstag und bin mit meiner Familie zu einem bekannten italienischen Restaurant in der nächsten Stadt gefahren, um zu feiern.
Es gab viele Probleme! Zuerst war der Tisch zu klein für sechs Personen. Wir haben lange auf einen anderen Tisch gewartet. Dann haben sie vergessen, das Essen für meinen kleinen Bruder zu bringen. Das Essen war auch nicht fantastisch, und mein Fisch war zu kalt. Wir waren wirklich enttäuscht.
Ich kann dieses Restaurant wirklich nicht empfehlen. Meiner Meinung nach werden wir nie wieder dort essen.

62. Lost property
1   (a) B
    (b) E
    (c) A
    (d) F
2   Letzte Woche am Dienstag bin ich mit dem Zug von Köln nach München gefahren.
    Leider, weil ich so müde war, bin ich eingeschlafen.
    Ich habe mein Handy in dem Zug gelassen / vergessen.
    Am nächsten Morgen bin ich zum Bahnhof zurückgegangen.
    Ich hatte Glück, weil jemand mein Handy gefunden (hat) und es ins Büro gebracht hat / denn jemand hat mein Handy gefunden.

63. Holiday jobs
1   (a) B
    (b) C
    (c) B
2   (a) fourteen / 14
    (b) helpful
    (c) restaurant
    (d) vocabulary / words

64. Buying gifts and souvenirs
1   (a) A 4
    (b) D 2
2   Sample answers:
    1 Eine junge Frau steht vor einem Geschäft.
    2 Ich denke, sie kauft eine Postkarte.
    3 Sie ist vielleicht im Urlaub.
    4 Sie trägt Sommerkleidung.
    5 Sie hat lange braune Haare.

65. Mobile technology
1   (a) A   (b) F   (c) B   (d) E
2   1 Ich finde die Technologie nützlich.
    2 Ich lade Bilder von meiner **Tätowierung** hoch.
    3 Es macht Spaß, soziale Netzwerke zu benutzen.
    4 Für Erdkunde suche ich Information über **Vulkane**.
    5 Es gibt nichts Interessanteres.

66. Social media
1   Sample answer:
Mein Handy ist toll und ganz neu. Es ist ein iPhone.
Ich finde die sozialen Medien lustig. Ich bin mit Freunden in Kontakt.
Das Internet ist nützlich, wenn ich Hausaufgaben mache.
Freunde teilen Fotos online, und ich sehe gern die Fotos.
Ich höre Musik auf meinem Handy, wenn ich zur Schule fahre.
2   Sample answer:
Ich benutze nicht sehr oft die sozialen Medien, aber manchmal gehe ich auf Instagram, wo es viele lustige Fotos gibt. Ich finde WhatsApp nützlich, um mit meinen Freunden und Freudinnen in Kontakt zu bleiben, besonders wenn sie nicht mehr in der Nähe wohnen.
Letzte Woche habe ich Fotos von unserem letzten Fußballspiel heruntergeladen. Es war unser bestes Spiel dieses Jahr. Es war toll, die Fotos zu sehen.
In der Zukunft werde ich mein Passwort regelmäßiger ändern, damit ich meine privaten Informationen schützen kann. Ich werde vorsichtig sein, welche Online-Freunde ich akzeptiere.

67. Internet
1   Sample answer:
Auf dem Foto gibt es ein Mädchen, das in der Schule arbeitet. Sie macht vielleicht Hausaufgaben. Sie schreibt und hat ein Tablet in einer Hand und Bücher und Papier auf dem Tisch. Hinter ihr sind auch viele Bücher. Das Mädchen hat lange dunkelblonde Haare und trägt ein weißes Hemd. Sie sieht ernst aus.

Hier gibt es drei Jugendliche, einen Jungen und zwei Mädchen. Sie sitzen im Wohnzimmer zu Hause. Ich sehe eine Pflanze. Ich denke, sie sehen einen Film im Internet an. Vielleicht ist das ein Horrorfilm, denn sie sehen überrascht aus. Der Junge hat kurze braune Haare und trägt ein T-Shirt. Beide Mädchen haben lange Haare.
Sample answers to follow-on questions:
    (a) Ich benutze jeden Tag das Internet, in der Schule und auch zu Hause. Ich finde es sehr nützlich.
    (b) Ich habe gestern eine Webseite für Fremdsprachen besucht. Die Webseite heißt Duolingo, und ich mag sie sehr.
    (c) Ich sehe gern Filme online an, denn man kann immer einen guten Film finden. Am liebsten sehe ich Krimis.
2   I find the internet necessary. / I think that the internet is necessary.
    We have a new computer at home.
    My parents think (that) I spend too much time online.
    Yesterday I downloaded a film.
    When / If I have time, I like playing video / computer games.

68. Computer games
1 Sample answer:
Ich mag Computerspiele und spiele jeden Tag Videospiele, entweder allein oder mit Freunden. Im Internet kann man viele spannende Spiele finden und man kann mit anderen Jugendlichen online spielen.
Ich habe aber einige Freunde, die zu viel Zeit beim Online-Spielen verbringen. Das heißt, dass sie in ihrem Zimmer bleiben und nicht mehr ausgehen, um Freunde zu treffen. Das kann nicht gesund sein.
Gestern habe ich mit meinem Bruder „Minecraft" gespielt. Das hat Spaß gemacht.
Ich möchte in der Zukunft die neue Version von „SuperMario" spielen. Die sieht sehr toll aus!
2 (a) complex games / games needing thought
  (b) war games

69. Opinions about technology
1 Sample answers:
  1 Auf dem Foto gibt es fünf Jugendliche, zwei Jungen und drei Mädchen.
  2 Sie sitzen in einem Garten oder in einem Park.
  3 Sie haben alle ein Laptop oder ein Tablet.
  4 Das Wetter ist schön und warm.
  5 Sie sind glücklich.
2 Sample answer:
Ich benutze jeden Tag Technologie, entweder mein Handy, einen Computer in der Schule oder mein Laptop zu Hause. Das Leben ohne digitale Geräte würde nicht mehr möglich sein. Ich schicke zum Beispiel viele SMS-Nachrichten, ich lade Filme herunter und ich spiele Computerspiele.
Diese sind einige Vorteile, aber es gibt andere positive Aspekte. Meine Eltern können jetzt oft von zu Hause arbeiten, und wir sehen uns mehr, und manchmal finde ich es praktischer, etwas online zu kaufen. Auf der anderen Seite gibt es Risiken, und man muss online immer vorsichtig sein.
In der Zukunft hoffe ich, auch von zu Hause arbeiten zu können und nicht jeden Tag in ein Büro fahren zu müssen. Das würde mir gefallen, weil ich besser arbeiten und mehr schaffen könnte, wenn ich nicht täglich vierzig Minuten mit dem Bus in die Stadt fahren müsste. Die Technologie wird auch eine größere Rolle in unseren Krankenhäusern spielen.

70. Films on the internet
1 (a) A
  (b) A
  (c) C
  (d) B
2 Sample answer:
In the twenty-first century, we no longer need traditional television.
It's / That's now very old technology.
Today, we have the internet and the possibility to watch / of watching all types of programmes.
With Netflix, you can watch what you like and also choose the time.
Yesterday, I watched an interesting film about jobs for young people.

71. My home
1 Mein Haus ist ziemlich modern.
  Es gibt eine große Küche.
  Ich mag mein Schlafzimmer, denn es ist bequem.
  Am Abend sehen wir oft einen Film.
  Letztes Wochenende hat er in dem / im Garten gearbeitet.
2 1 Ich wohne in einem Haus in der Stadt.
  2 Unser Haus hat drei **Stockwerke**.
  3 Ich mag es hier, weil es ruhig ist.
  4 Oben gibt es einen **Dachboden**.
  5 Mein Schlafzimmer ist bequem.

72. My town
1 Sample answers:
  1 Ich sehe fünf Mädchen.
  2 Sie sind in der Stadt.
  3 Es regnet und ist kalt.
  4 Ein Mädchen trägt eine schwarze Jacke.
  5 Es gibt ein Geschäft.
2 (a) A
  (b) A+B
  (c) A

73. Facilities in town
1 Sample answer:
Auf dem ersten Foto sehe ich viele Leute in einer historischen Stadtmitte. Ich denke, die Stadt ist klein, weil die Straße sehr eng ist. Es gibt dort keine Autos, und alle gehen zu Fuß einkaufen. Sie tragen Sommerkleidung, also denke ich, dass das Wetter warm und sonnig ist. Einige Leute haben etwas gekauft und tragen Taschen.
Ich sehe auf dem zweiten Foto vier Jugendliche, die in der Stadt sind. Ich denke, sie gehen zusammen einkaufen. Die beiden Mädchen tragen Taschen und haben schon etwas gekauft. Die Mädchen sehen glücklich aus. Ein Mädchen trägt einen Rock und ein weißes T-Shirt. Das andere Mädchen trägt rote Schuhe. Ich denke, das Wetter ist gut, weil sie keine Jacken tragen.
Sample answers to follow-on questions:
(a) Ich mag meine Stadt, obwohl sie ein bisschen klein ist. Es gibt aber ziemlich viel für Jugendliche, was toll ist, weil das Leben nie langweilig ist.
(b) Letzten Samstag bin ich mit meiner Freundin einkaufen gegangen. Ich habe ein T-Shirt gekauft, weil ich neue Kleidung für eine Party haben wollte. Danach haben wir im Café gegessen.
(c) Ich werde am Samstag für die nächste Prüfung lernen, aber am Sonntag will ich mich mit meinen Freundinnen treffen. Wir werden bei mir einen Film ansehen.
2 (a) Willst
  (b) modernes
  (c) kauft
  (d) dem
  (e) Ich

74. Finding the way
1 (a) D / 1
  (b) B / 4
  (c) C / 2
2 (a) C (b) C (c) A (d) C (e) B (f) A

75. Shops and shopping
1 Sample answers:
  1 Es gibt einen jungen Mann.
  2 Er ist in einem Geschäft.
  3 Er trägt ein schwarzes T-Shirt.
  4 Er sieht ein Hemd an.
  5 Er mag das Hemd und ist glücklich.
2 Sample answer:
Auf dem ersten Foto gibt es eine junge Frau in einem Buchladen. Sie hat blonde Haare und trägt eine Brille. Sie trägt eine warme Jacke – es ist vielleicht Winter. Sie sieht ein Buch an, und ich denke, sie findet es interessant und wird es kaufen.
Auf dem zweiten Foto gibt es eine junge Frau, die einkaufen geht. Sie ist in einem Kleidungsgeschäft. Die Frau hat lange Haare und trägt eine Hose und ein weißes Hemd. Sie hat ihre Handtasche mit. Ich denke, sie mag die Kleidung, denn sie sieht glücklich aus.

Sample answers to follow-on questions:
(a) Ich kaufe nicht oft Bücher, weil ich meistens online lese. Wir haben viele Bücher zu Hause, weil meine Eltern gern lesen.
(b) Ich habe letzte Woche einen neuen Rock gekauft und auch eine Hose. Die habe ich auf dem Markt gefunden, und sie waren ziemlich billig.
(c) Mein Traum ist, eine Handtasche von Céline zu haben. Das ist eine französische Marke. Die Produkte sind aber sehr teuer.

76. Shopping in town
1 (a) D
  (b) A
  (c) E
  (d) C
2 1 Es gibt am Samstagmorgen einen Markt.
  2 An einigen **Ständen** gibt es verschiedenes Essen.
  3 Einer der Verkäufer hat schöne **Lederwaren**.
  4 Gestern habe ich eine Handtasche gekauft.
  5 Sie war nicht teuer.

77. Transport
1 Sample answer:
In meiner Stadt gibt es öffentliche Verkehrsmittel. Es gibt regelmäßig Busse, aber wir haben keinen Bahnhof und keine U-Bahn. Ich gehe meistens zu Fuß zur Schule, weil es nicht sehr weit ist. Wenn es regnet, fahre ich manchmal mit dem Bus. Gestern bin ich mit meiner Mutter mit dem Auto in die Stadt gefahren, um einkaufen zu gehen. Das war praktisch und viel schneller als mit dem Bus.
In den Ferien werden wir mit dem Zug zum Flughafen fahren und dann nach Spanien fliegen, obwohl ich weiß, dass Fliegen nicht umweltfreundlich ist.
2 Public transport in my area is awful.
The reason for this is that I live in a village in the countryside.
There are few buses and so we have to use the car.
Yesterday my brother drove me to school.
It was raining hard and I couldn't go by bike.

78. Travelling by train
1 (a) C   (b) A   (c) B   (d) C
2 (a) B   (b) A   (c) A+B   (d) A

79. The environment and me
1 Sample answer:
Teacher: Du sprichst mit deiner deutschen Freundin. Ich bin deine Freundin.

Teacher: Wie findest du die Umwelt in deiner Stadt?
Student: Ich denke, es gibt zu viele Autos in der Stadt. Die Luft ist schmutzig.
Teacher: Das ist ein Problem.
Student: Was ist für dich das größte Problem?
Teacher: Das schlimmste Problem ist der Müll.
Teacher: Warum ist die Umwelt wichtig für dich?
Student: Wir haben nur eine Welt und müssen auf sie aufpassen.
Teacher: Stimmt.
Teacher: Was hast du in letzter Zeit gemacht, was umweltfreundlich ist?
Student: Ich bin immer zu Fuß gegangen und habe Müll recycelt.
Teacher: Gut.
Teacher: Wie wirst du in der Zukunft die Umwelt schützen?
Student: Ich werde in der Stadt Müll sammeln.
Teacher: Gute Idee.
2 1 Die Stadt ist nicht sauber.
  2 **Lärm** ist ein großes Problem.
  3 Es gibt **Abfall** in dem Park.
  4 Ich bin immer umweltfreundlich.

80. Environmental problems
1 Reading aloud text and sample answer to follow-on questions:
(a) Die Umwelt ist nicht schlecht, aber es gibt viel Müll in der Stadt.
(b) Ich recycle Papier und Glas.
(c) Es wird in der Zukunft nicht genug Wasser geben.
(d) Ich fahre nicht oft mit dem Auto. Es ist besser, mit dem Fahrrad zu fahren.

2 Sample answer:
Auf dem Foto gibt es einen Mann. Er ist auf dem Land und geht durch ein Feld. Er trägt eine Hose und ein T-Shirt. Das Foto ist in zwei Teilen. Auf der rechten Seite ist die Welt schön. Der Himmel ist blau, und das Gras ist grün. Auf der linken Seite ist alles braun und trocken, weil die Welt zu warm ist. Es gibt kein Gras mehr. Das ist der Klimawandel.

Sample answers to follow-on questions:
(a) Das Hauptproblem ist der Klimawandel. Die Welt wird wärmer.
(b) Ich habe zu Hause Glas, Papier und Plastik recycelt und habe nicht zu viel Wasser benutzt.
(c) Ich werde nie mehr mit dem Flugzeug fliegen und ich werde kein Auto fahren. Ich werde versuchen, Energie zu sparen.

81. The dangers of pollution
1 1 Wir möchten Energie sparen.
  2 Ich **dusche** jeden Tag.
  3 Zu Hause recycelt meine Mutter **Plastik**.
  4 Ich will die Umwelt schützen.
2 Sample answer:
Auf dem ersten Foto gibt es drei junge Leute, einen Mann und zwei Frauen. Der Mann rechts hat kurze, schwarze Haare. Sie tragen alle grüne T-Shirts. Sie lächeln, aber sie konzentrieren sich. Sie sind in einem Park oder vielleicht in einem Garten. Der Boden ist schmutzig. Ich denke, das Wetter ist warm. Sie sammeln Papier, um der Umwelt zu helfen.

Auf dem zweiten Foto sehe ich eine Frau mit ihren Kindern und mit einem Hund. Sie sind traurig, weil sie die Umweltverschmutzung in der Stadt sehen. Es gibt viele Fabriken. Sie verschmutzen die Luft und das Meer.

82. Individual actions for the environment
1 Sample answer:
Es gibt heute viele Probleme mit der Umwelt. Ich versuche, die Luft nicht zu verschmutzen, denn ich gehe zu Fuß oder fahre mit dem Fahrrad. Zu Hause spare ich Energie und Wasser. Wir sollen alle etwas machen, um die Umwelt zu schützen.
In letzter Zeit habe ich jeden Tag den Müll zu Hause getrennt. Ich habe Glas, Plastik und Papier recycelt. Wenn alle Leute das machen, gibt es weniger Müll.
In Zukunft werde ich nicht mit dem Flugzeug fliegen, weil das nicht umweltfreundlich ist, und ich werde auch kein Auto kaufen.
2 Reading aloud text and sample answer to follow-on questions:
(a) Ich habe Angst, dass die Welt zu heiß wird, und dass es kein Wasser gibt.
(b) Ich habe Plastik, Glas und Papier recycelt und bin nicht mit dem Auto gefahren.

151

(c) Man wird nicht mehr fliegen, nie Müll liegen lassen und weniger Energie benutzen.
(d) Die Umwelt hier ist nicht schlecht, obwohl das Stadtzentrum oft schmutzig ist. Die Leute sind zu faul, ihren Müll mit nach Hause zu nehmen.

83. How to recycle
1 Sample answers:
   1 Ich sehe vier Kinder.
   2 Es gibt zwei Jungen und zwei Mädchen.
   3 Sie sind zu Hause in dem Garten.
   4 Das Wetter ist schön.
   5 Sie recyceln Flaschen.
2 Sample answers:
Ich interessiere mich für die Umwelt und will sie schützen.
Deshalb trenne ich immer den Müll zu Hause und werfe Papier in den blauen Sack.
Es ist nicht schwierig, und alle sollen es machen / tun.
Wenn man das macht, kann man viele Sachen recyceln.
Gestern habe ich mit einer Gruppe zusammen gearbeitet, um den Park sauber zu machen.

84. Weather
1 Sample answers:
   1 Es gibt einen Mann und eine Frau.
   2 Sie haben ein kleines Kind.
   3 Der Hund ist schwarz und weiß.
   4 Sie sind im Park.
   5 Das Wetter ist schön.
2 (a) rain
   (b) cold
   (c) snow
   (d) closed

85. The natural world
1 I live in a village in the country.
The fresh air is healthy.
In my area there are lots of trees. Last weekend, we went for a walk / hike in the wood(s) / forest.
I like living here.
2 (a) sea
   (b) airport
   (c) concerts
   (d) walking / hiking / cycle
   (e) safe

86. Practice for Paper 1: Listening
1 1.1 B
   1.2 A
   1.3 B
   1.4 C
2 1 Ich suche ein Geschenk für meine Schwester.
   2 Was kostet die Bluse?
   3 Welche Größe ist das Kleid?
   4 Die Handschuhe gefallen mir.

87. Practice for Paper 1: Listening
1 1 Lara: likes B / dislikes C
   2 Arda: likes E / dislikes A
2 1 Dieses Jahr ist Biologie mein Lieblingsfach.
   2 Mein Mathelehrer ist häufig schlecht **gelaunt**.
   3 Ich würde lieber **Informatik** lernen.
   4 Nächstes Jahr gehe ich in die Oberstufe.
   5 Da kann ich meine Fächer wählen.

88. Practice for Paper 2: Speaking
Role play
Teacher: Du sprichst mit deiner deutschen Freundin. Ich bin deine Freundin.
Teacher: Was machst du in deiner Freizeit?

 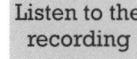

Student: Ich spiele Computerspiele mit meinen Freunden.
Teacher: Toll.
Teacher: Wie findest du Musik?
Student: Ich liebe Rap und Rockmusik, aber ich mag klassische Musik nicht.
Teacher: Schön.
Student: Was machst du in deiner Freizeit?
Teacher: Ich spiele Tennis.
Teacher: Wie oft gehst du ins Kino?
Student: Ich gehe einmal im Monat ins Kino.
Teacher: Gut.
Teacher: Welche Pläne hast du für dieses Wochenende?
Student: Ich werde mit Freunden Fußball spielen.
Teacher: Gute Idee.

Reading aloud and sample answers to follow-on questions:
(a) Meine Stadt ist ziemlich schmutzig, denn es gibt viele Autos.
(b) Ich komme gern zu Fuß zur Schule. Das ist gut für mich und für die Umwelt.
(c) Ich recycle Glas und Papier und ich spare Energie.
(d) Ich kaufe sehr oft recyceltes Papier für die Schule.

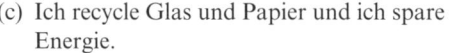

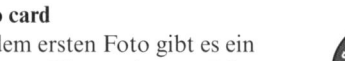

Photo card
Auf dem ersten Foto gibt es ein modernes Klassenzimmer. Die Fenster sind groß. Ich sehe eine junge Lehrerin und sieben Schüler in dem Zimmer. Es gibt drei Mädchen und vier Jungen. Sie tragen keine Uniform. Sie lesen und schreiben. Ich denke, das ist eine Englischstunde.
Ich sehe auf dem zweiten Foto fünf Schüler – es gibt Mädchen und Jungen. Sie spielen Basketball draußen in der Nähe von der Schule. Das Wetter ist ziemlich gut, und sie tragen T-Shirts. Es ist vielleicht die Pause oder die Mittagspause. Die Schule ist modern und hat große Fenster.

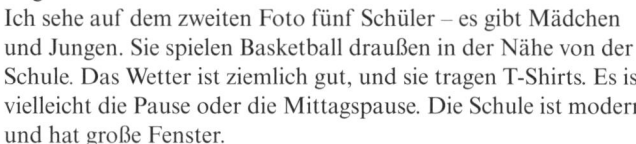

Sample answers to follow-on questions:
(Present tense)
(a) Meine Schule ist gut and sehr modern. Es gibt tausend Schüler und Schülerinnen, und ich denke, die Schule ist zu groß.
(b) Mein Lieblingsfach ist Mathe, denn ich habe einen sehr guten Lehrer und ich finde die Stunden interessant. Ich verstehe das Fach und habe gute Noten.
(c) Meiner Meinung nach ist der Tag zu lang und er beginnt zu früh. Wir sind immer müde.
(d) Meine Lehrer sind gut und freundlich.
(Past tense)
(e) Gestern habe ich Mathe gelernt.
(f) Ich habe Fußball gespielt.
(g) Wir sind nach Manchester gefahren. Das war toll.
(Future tense)
(h) Nächstes Jahr möchte ich Fremdsprachen und Mathe lernen. Das sind meine Lieblingsfächer.
(i) Ich möchte auf die Uni gehen und Biologie studieren.
(j) Ich will bei einer Bank arbeiten.

89. Practice for Paper 2: Speaking
Role play
Teacher: Du sprichst mit deiner schweizerischen Freundin. Ich bin deine Freundin.
Teacher: Wie oft treibst du Sport?
Student: Ich spiele montags Tennis und am Samstag habe ich immer ein Fußballspiel.
Teacher: Sehr gut.

Teacher: Warum ist dir Sport wichtig?
Student: Ich will fit und gesund bleiben, und Sport hilft mir dabei. Bewegung macht mich auch glücklich.
Teacher: Interessant.
Teacher: Wie findest du Computerspiele?
Student: Computerspiele haben für mich keinen Sinn. Ich denke, es ist ungesund, immer in seinem Zimmer zu sitzen.
Teacher: Alles klar.
Teacher: Was wirst du heute Abend essen und trinken?
Student: Ich werde Hähnchen essen und Wasser trinken.
Teacher: Gut.
Student: Lebst du gesund?
Teacher: Ja, ich lebe sehr gesund.

Reading aloud and sample answers to follow-on questions:
(a) Ich gehe morgens gern laufen. Im Sommer spiele ich Tennis und gehe schwimmen.
(b) Ich mag Teamsport mit Freunden und spiele oft Fußball. Das macht viel Spaß.
(c) Ich esse gesund, und ich mag Obst und Gemüse. Ich trinke auch regelmäßig Wasser. Ich trinke auch nie Alkohol.
(d) Ich finde Rauchen blöd und ich verstehe nicht, warum viele junge Leute rauchen wollen. Es ist teuer und gefährlich.

Photo card
Auf dem ersten Foto gibt es vier Mädchen. Sie gehen in dem Park zusammen spazieren. Alles ist grün und es gibt große Bäume. Das Wetter ist sonnig. Jedes Mädchen hat ein Handy und spricht mit jemandem. Es ist komisch, denn sie sprechen nicht miteinander. Es gibt auf dem zweiten Foto vier Jugendliche, zwei Jungen und zwei Mädchen. Ich denke, sie sind in der Schule, denn es gibt viele Bücher. Vielleicht machen sie Schularbeit oder Hausaufgaben zusammen. Sie benutzen Tablets, um mit der Arbeit zu helfen.

Sample answers to follow-on questions:
(Present tense)
(a) Mein Handy ist absolut nötig für mein Leben. Ohne mein Handy bin ich verloren.
(b) Ich finde Infos für meine Hausaufgaben im Internet. Ich will für Erdkunde etwas über die Umwelt in Südamerika herausfinden.
(c) Ich mag Facebook nicht, weil ich denke, es ist für ältere Leute. Instagram und Snapchat sind manchmal lustig, aber manchmal blöd.
(Past tense)
(d) Ich habe auf einer Modewebseite eine neue Hose gekauft. Dann habe ich eine E-Mail geschickt, weil meine Freundin in Amerika Geburtstag hatte.
(e) Ich habe keine Probleme mit den sozialen Medien gehabt, aber ich weiß, dass es manchmal Probleme gibt.
(f) Ja. Ich kaufe oft online, denn es ist oft billiger als in einem Geschäft. Ich habe gestern ein Buch bei Amazon gekauft.
(g) Computerspiele finde ich nicht interessant. Ich habe neulich Filme heruntergeladen. Das finde ich besser als Videospiele.
(Future tense)
(h) Ich werde mit Freunden sprechen und Fotos auf Instagram hochladen.
(i) Ich möchte nächste Woche eine neue Jacke und eine Hose online kaufen.
(j) Ich würde sehr gern den neuen Film „Vanya" mit Andrew Scott sehen, aber ich muss warten, bis der Film online ist, dann werde ich ihn herunterladen.

90. Practice for Paper 3: Reading
1
 1 A
 2 A
 3 B
 4 C
2 I am healthy.
 I eat fruit and vegetables every day.
 Once a week I go to the gym.
 Yesterday I had / did a dance class.
 I am happier, when / if I do activity / take exercise.

91. Practice for Paper 3: Reading
1
 1 It's suffering.
 2 Forests are being destroyed. / Animal species are disappearing.
 3 carrying on as if everything is OK
 4 changing our lifestyles
2 Sample responses:
When school is over / finished, I would like to go to university to study.
My favourite subject is history because I'm interested in the events of the past.
I am looking forward to leaving my town,
Life here can be rather boring and I need new experiences.
I hope to meet lots of new people.

92. Practice for Paper 4: Writing
1 Sample answer:
Meine Stadt ist nicht sehr groß.
Es gibt Geschäfte, ein Kino und einen schönen Park.
Die Umwelt ist sauber, und es gibt nicht zu viele Autos.
Man kann zu Fuß gehen, denn die Stadt ist klein, aber es gibt auch Busse.
Die Gegend ist grün, und es gibt einen Wald.
2 Sample answer:
Meine Schule ist sehr alt, aber nicht groß. Die Schule sieht nicht sehr schön aus, aber die Klassenzimmer sind warm und bequem.
Ich finde meine Schule toll, weil ich viel Freunde habe und die Lehrer und Lehrerinnen freundlich sind.
Letzten Monat haben wir mit meiner Kunstklasse eine Reise nach London gemacht. Wir haben ein Kunstmuseum besucht. Das war toll, und ich habe viel über Mark Rothko gelernt.
Nächstes Jahr möchte ich in der Schule bleiben. Ich will Englisch, Musik und Deutsch lernen, denn das sind meine Lieblingsfächer.
Ich hoffe, ich bekomme in den Prüfungen gute Noten.

93. Practice for Paper 4: Writing
1 Sample answer:
Ich versuche immer, gesund zu essen und genug zu schlafen. Jeden Tag esse ich Gemüse und Obst und ich trinke viel Wasser. Ich denke, ich bin sehr aktiv.
Ich bin sehr sportlich und liebe Fußball und Tennis. Ich finde Sport sehr positiv, weil ich mit Freunden spiele, und das macht Spaß.
Letzte Woche bin ich zweimal schwimmen gegangen, weil das Wetter so schön war. Ich bin auch mit dem Fahrrad zur Schule gefahren. Das ist schneller, als zu Fuß zu gehen.
In Zukunft werde ich Mitglied in einem Fitnesszentrum werden.
2 Sample answer:
Ich benutze jeden Tag mein Handy, um mit Freunden in Kontakt zu bleiben. Ich finde es auch nützlich, um Musik zu hören und Videos zu sehen.
Ich finde diese schnelle Kommunikation toll. Heute kann man viel machen, was früher nicht möglich war.
Das Internet kann nützlich sein, wenn man für Hausaufgaben Informationen braucht, oder etwas kaufen will.
Die negative Seite ist, dass es Gefahren gibt. Deshalb muss man online immer aufpassen und keine persönlichen Daten mit fremden Leuten teilen.

Ich benutze nicht oft soziale Netzwerke. Ich finde Facebook nicht sehr interessant. Instagram und Snapchat sind besser. Mit Instagram sehe ich, was meine Freunde machen und ich habe gestern Fotos hochgeladen.
In Zukunft werde ich immer online einkaufen und werde nie in den Supermarkt gehen. Ich werde später hoffentlich zu Hause arbeiten können und nicht jeden Tag ins Büro fahren müssen. Das wäre ein großer Vorteil, besonders wenn ich Kinder habe.

94. Gender and plurals
1 (a) das (b) der (c) die (d) das (e) das
  (f) die (g) der (h) die
2 (a) Die (b) Das (c) Das (d) Der (e) Der (f) Die
3 (a) pl (b) sg (c) pl (d) sg / pl (e) pl (f) sg
  (g) sg (h) pl (i) sg (j) sg / pl

95. Indefinite articles and possessives
1 (a) ein (b) eine (c) ein (d) ein (e) eine
  (f) ein (g) eine (h) ein (i) ein (j) ein
2 (a) kein (b) kein (c) keine (d) kein (e) keine
3 (a) meine Schwester (b) deine Familie (c) seine Frau
  (d) ihr Freund (e) unsere Stadt (f) meine Hausaufgaben
  (g) seine Jacke (h) ihre Party (i) deine Kleidung
  (j) mein Glas

96. Nominative and accusative cases
1 (a) Der (b) Das / den (c) Der / das (d) Die / die
  (e) Die / den (f) Die / das (g) Der / die (h) Die / das
2 (a) einen (b) ein (c) einen (d) einen (e) einen (f) ein
3 (a) Meine (b) dein (c) Mein / seine (d) Ihr (e) unser
  (f) Meine

97. Other cases and prepositions
1 (a) der Lehrerin (b) dem Haus (c) seiner Mutter
  (d) meinem Vater (e) ihren Freunden (f) meinen Eltern
2 (a) abroad / overseas (b) on / at the coast
  (c) in the country(side) (d) at our house
  (e) on the contrary
3 (a) des Mädchens (b) der Stadt (c) des Wetters
  (d) der Sommerferien (e) der Ärzte
4 (a) The girl's brother is quite sporty.
  (b) In the middle of the town is a market.
  (c) In spite of the weather we are going camping.
  (d) During the summer holidays, I play basketball.
  (e) The work of the doctors is very hard. / The doctors' work is very hard.

98. Prepositions with the accusative or dative
1 (a) in die Stadt (b) in dem Garten
  (c) in dem Meer (d) auf dem Tisch
  (e) an der Wand (f) in das Haus
  (g) neben dem Fluss (h) unter dem Baum
  (i) unter das Bett (j) hinter dem Fitness-Studio
  (k) vor den Computer (l) zwischen dem Kino und der Schule
2 (a) das (b) den (c) die
3 (a) My sister and I talk about the problem.
  (b) I'm waiting for the next train.
  (c) The students are thinking about the future.

99. *Dieser, jeder* and *welcher*
1 (a) Diese (b) jeder (c) diesen (d) diese (e) Welche
  (f) Dieser (g) dieses (h) Welcher (i) diesem (j) diesem
2 (a) Welchen (b) welchem (c) diesem (d) Diese
  (e) dieses (f) dieses (g) Jede (h) Jeder (i) Jede
  (j) jedem (k) Jedes (l) jedes
3 (a) jedes (b) diese (c) diesen (d) jedes (e) jeden

100. Adjective endings
1 (a) schwarze (b) neuen (c) weißen (d) braunen
  (e) bekannte
2 (a) kleiner (b) ältere (c) interessantes (d) gesundes
  (e) kleine (f) besten
3 (a) schwarzen (b) frisches (c) freundliche (d) weißen

101. Comparative and superlative adjectives and adverbs
1 (a) interessanter (b) intelligenter (c) schneller
  (d) kleiner
2 (a) modernste (b) schwerste (c) langsamste
  (d) teuerste
3 (a) schöner / am schönsten (b) schneller / am schnellsten
4 (a) My father is taller than me / I am.
  (b) What is the highest mountain in Switzerland called?
  (c) What sort of films do you like watching the most?

102. Personal pronouns
1 (a) du (b) uns (c) ihr (d) mir (e) Ihnen (f) dich
  (g) sie (h) ihm (i) sie (j) dir
2 (a) euch (b) uns (c) mir (d) ihm (e) dir (f) ihr

103. Word order 1
1 (a) Nächstes Jahr fahren wir in die Schweiz.
  (b) Jeden Morgen geht mein Bruder im Park laufen.
  (c) In der Schule lerne ich sehr gerne Englisch.
  (d) In den Ferien spielen meine Freunde Fußball.
2 (a) Letzte Woche hat mein Freund eine Party gehabt.
  (b) Plötzlich ist die Katze aus dem Fenster gesprungen.
  (c) Wir sind wegen des Wetters spät in Berlin angekommen.
3 (a) Er wird morgen Golf spielen.
  (b) Wann wirst du einkaufen gehen?
  (c) Nächstes Jahr werde ich die Schule verlassen.
4 (a) Ich muss zuerst meine Hausaufgaben machen.
  (b) Meine Schwester will nach London fahren.
  (c) Bald können wir endlich mehr Freizeit haben.

104. Conjunctions
1 (a) Wir bleiben diesen Sommer zu Hause, weil Reisen sehr teuer ist.
  (b) Ich will in der Zukunft studieren, weil ich Arzt werden will.
  (c) Er geht auf dem Land wandern, weil das Wetter schön ist.
  (d) Mein Bruder geht zu jedem Fußballspiel, weil er ein großer Fan ist.
  (e) Wir sollen die Umwelt besser schützen, weil es nur eine Welt gibt.
2 (a) Es war sehr spät, als ich nach Hause gekommen bin.
  (b) Bevor er zur Arbeit geht, isst er das Frühstück.
  (c) Die Lehrerin hilft uns, damit wir besser verstehen.
  (d) Wir wollten ausgehen, da ich Geburtstag hatte.
  (e) Die Studenten wissen, dass sie hart arbeiten müssen.
3 (a) It was very late when I got home.
  (b) Before he goes to work, he has breakfast.
  (c) The teacher helps us, so that we understand better.
  (d) We wanted to go out, as it was my birthday.
  (e) The students know that they have to work hard.

105. Word order 2
1 (a) Wir fahren dieses Jahr in den Urlaub, um die Sonne zu genießen.
  (b) Ich werde nach London fahren, um eine Arbeitsstelle zu suchen.
  (c) Er fährt auf dem Land Fahrrad, um an der frischen Luft zu sein.
2 (a) Ich hoffe, nächstes Jahr ein Auslandsjahr zu machen.
  (b) Wir versuchen, gesünder zu leben.
  (c) Mein Freund beginnt, mehr Sport zu treiben.
3 (a) der (b) das (c) die (d) den (e) die

106. The present tense
1 (a) wohne (b) spielen (c) gehst (d) kauft (e) lachen (f) macht (g) kocht (h) Liebst (i) schicken (j) Besuchst (k) arbeitet (l) beginnt
2 (a) fährst (b) fahre (c) lesen (d) liest (e) spricht (f) gibt (g) schläft (h) trifft (i) trägt (j) hilft

107. Reflexive and separable verbs
1 (a) iii (b) vi (c) i (d) ii (e) iv (f) v
2 (a) uns (b) mich (c) sich (d) sich (e) uns (f) mich
3 (a) kommt … an (b) rufe … an (c) kommen … zurück (d) lade … herunter (e) gehen … aus
4 (a) zurückgekommen (b) angerufen (c) hochgeladen (d) angekommen (e) ferngesehen
5 (a) Ich werde morgen in der Schweiz ankommen.
   (b) Später wird er Musikvideos im Internet ansehen.
   (c) Meine Eltern werden morgen früh aufstehen.

108. Irregular verb tables 1
1 (a) isst (b) fährt (c) gibt (d) hast (e) hilft (f) läufst
2 Both tiers:
   (a) mochte (b) musste (c) gab (d) hatten (e) konnte
   Higher tier:
   (a) begann (b) blieb (c) kam (d) las (e) mussten
3 (a) bin / gegangen b) hast / gegessen (c) habe / gefunden

109. Irregular verb tables 2
1 (a) nehme (b) sieht (c) spricht (d) trägst (e) trifft (f) vergisst
2 Both tiers:
   (a) wollte (b) war (c) wollte (d) war (e) war
   Higher tier:
   (a) nahmen (b) ahen (c) schlief (d) saßen (e) sprach
3 (a) bin / geschwommen (b) hast / genommen (c) hat / gesehen (d) habe / vergessen

110. Using irregular verbs in different tenses
1 (a) singen (b) vergisst (c) sehen (d) mag (e) fährt (f) habe
2 (a) beginnt (b) schreibt (c) spricht (d) trägst (e) trinken
3 (a) hat … begonnen (b) hat … gegessen (c) bin … gegangen (d) hat … gewonnen (e) haben … gebracht (f) habe … gelesen (g) haben … geholfen (h) bin … gelaufen (i) sind … gekommen (j) hat … getrunken
4 Both tiers:
   (a) hatte (b) onnte (c) musste
   Higher tier:
   (a) trank (b) sprachen (c) gab

111. *Sein* and *haben*
1 (a) Hast (b) hat (c) habe (d) haben (e) sind (f) Bist (g) bin
2 (a) hatten (b) hatte (c) hatten (d) hatte (e) war (f) waren (g) war
3 (a) ist / gewesen (b) Hast / gehabt (c) bist / gewesen (d) sind / gewesen

112. Modal verbs in the present tense
1 (a) will (b) sollen (c) magst (d) darf (e) muss (f) können
2 (a) My brother wants to go to university.
   (b) We should protect the environment.
   (c) Which shirt do you like?
   (d) You're not allowed to smoke here.
   (e) I have to / must learn these words by tomorrow.
   (f) When can we visit you?
3 Both tiers:
   (a) mochte (b) sollte (c) musste (d) konnte
   Higher tier:
   (a) konnten (b) wolltet (c) durften

113. The perfect tense with *haben*
1 (a) habe / gespielt (b) Hat / gekauft (c) haben / geschickt (d) haben / gewartet (e) habe / gearbeitet (f) hat / gelernt
2 (a) gelesen (b) gegessen (c) getrunken (d) gesprochen (e) geholfen (f) geschrieben (g) getroffen (h) gegeben

114. The perfect tense with *sein*
1 (a) bin (b) bist (c) sind (d) ist (e) sind (f) ist (g) sind (h) bin (i) ist
2 (a) Bist du nach Berlin gefahren?
   (b) Wir sind gestern Abend spät angekommen.
   (c) Ich bin heute Morgen ins Fitness-Studio gegangen.
   (d) Sie sind krank gewesen.
   (e) Sie ist sportlicher geworden.

115. The imperfect tense
1 (a) spielte (b) lernten (c) diskutierten (d) kochte (e) malte (f) kaufte
2 Both tiers:
   (a) war (b) hatte (c) gab (d) musste (e) wollte (f) Hatten
   Higher tier:
   (a) lief (b) kam (c) konnten (d) blieb (e) aßen (f) schwammen (g) ging (h) gab (i) fuhr

116. The future tense
1 (a) wirst (b) werde (c) wird (d) werden (e) werden
2 (a) Mein Freund wird im Oktober auf die Uni gehen.
   (b) Ich denke, ich werde Tierärztin sein.
   (c) Wir werden nächstes Jahr eine Party haben.
   (d) Es wird in der Zukunft nicht genug Wasser geben.
   (e) Flugzeuge werden unsere Welt weiter zerstören.
3 (a) Next September, I'm going into the sixth form.
   (b) This evening, we want to eat with my grandparents.
   (c) In the future, I will definitely not get married.
4 (a) In der Zukunft möchte ich mit Tieren arbeiten.
   (b) Ich will Schauspieler sein.
   (c) Nächste Woche will ich neue Kleidung kaufen.

117. The conditional
1 (a) Ich würde Geschichte studieren.
   (b) Mein Bruder würde eine Lehre machen.
   (c) Unsere Lehrerin würde nicht zufrieden sein.
   (d) Was würden sie machen?
   (e) Vielleicht würde ich die Schule verlassen.
2 (a) I would leave school straight away if I was allowed to.
   (b) What would he do if he were / was rich?
   (c) I would spend a long holiday on an island.
   (d) If he could, my brother would live with his girlfriend.
   (e) If I were / was the headteacher, there would be no more homework.

118. Paper 1: Listening (Foundation)
1 E	2 D	3 A	4 F
5 B 1	6 D 3	7.1 P	7.2 P+N
8.1 B	8.2 A	8.3 C	9.1 C
9.2 A	10.1 N	10.2 P	10.3 F
11.1 C	11.2 A	11.3 B	11.4 B

12 helpful / explain
13 classrooms / uncomfortable
14 A 15 D 16 F 17 B
18.1 (His / Finn and Lena's) stepmother
18.2 Red trousers

Dictation
1. Ich spiele gern Fußball.
2. Mein Vater ist sehr sportlich.
3. Die **Bäckerei** ist in der Stadt.
4. Die Jungen gehen oft **tauchen**.

121. Paper 2: Speaking (Foundation)
1 Role play
Sample answer:
Teacher: Du sprichst mit deiner deutschen Freundin. Ich bin deine Freundin.
Teacher: Was machst du am Wochenende?
Student: Ich mache meine Hausaufgaben.
Teacher: Alles klar.
Teacher: Und wie oft machst du Sport?
Student: Ich spiele jeden Tag Fußball.
Teacher: Interessant.
Student: Wie findest du Fernsehen?
Teacher: Ich sehe gern fern.
Teacher: Wie findest du Filme im Kino?
Student: Ich sehe gern Filme im Kino.
Teacher: Interessant.
Teacher: Wie ist das Kino in deiner Stadt?
Student: Das Kino ist modern und teuer.
Teacher: Das stimmt.

2 Reading aloud and sample answers to follow-on questions:
(a) Ich habe vier gute Freunde in meiner Klasse. Sie sind alle nett. Wir machen viel zusammen.
(b) Ich mache gern Sport mit Freunden. Nach der Schule spielen wir oft Fußball in dem Park. Wir gehen am Wochenende aus.
(c) Meine beste Freundin ist klein und sportlich. Sie hat lange braune Haare und ist schön.
(d) Ich gehe nicht gern einkaufen, aber ich gehe trotzdem mit meiner Freundin in die Stadt. Sie liebt die Geschäfte.

3 Photo card
Sample answer:
Ich sehe sechs junge Leute. Sie spielen Basketball. Es gibt drei Mädchen und drei Jungen. Ich denke, es ist Sommer. Das Wetter ist schön, und der Himmel ist blau. Sie tragen T-Shirts. Sie sind in einem Park.

Es gibt fünf Jugendliche. Sie sind zu Hause und essen Pizza. Es gibt zwei Mädchen und drei Jungen. Die Mädchen haben lange blonde Haare, und die Jungen haben kurze Haare. Sie sind glücklich und haben Spaß zusammen.
Sample answers to follow-on questions:
(a) Ich mag Sport und ich bin sehr sportlich. Mein Lieblingssport ist Tennis.
(b) In der Schule spielen wir Fußball und wir schwimmen und laufen.
(c) Ich trinke Wasser und ich esse Obst. Ich rauche nicht.
(d) Mein Lieblingsessen ist Fisch mit Pommes. Das ist lecker, aber nicht sehr gesund.
(e) Heute Morgen habe ich Brot mit Käse gegessen und ich habe Kaffee getrunken.
(f) Ich finde Rauchen blöd. Es ist teuer und sehr schlecht für die Gesundheit.
(g) Ich spiele gern mit meinen Freunden Tennis oder Fußball. Wir gehen manchmal einkaufen oder sehen einen Film an.
(h) Dieses Wochenende werden wir ausgehen. Es gibt ein Konzert in der Stadt. Das wird Spaß machen.
(i) Ich habe Hausaufgaben gemacht und Musik gehört.
(j) Ich esse nicht oft in einem Restaurant. Es ist teuer.

122. Paper 3: Reading (Foundation)
1 E 2 A 3 D 4 B
5 T 6 A 7 F 8 F
9 A 10 T 11 P+N 12 N
13 P 14 P 15 A 16 B
17 B 18 C 19 C 20.1 F
20.2 P 20.3 N
21 He has a lot of homework. / He has to help his mum.
22 He walks to school.
23 He goes shopping (for the family).
24 His brother will join him / do sport with him.
25 D 26 E 27 B 28 A
29 She was 17.
30 She began to train as an actor.
31 best young actress
32 an action thriller
33 A 34 B / C 35 3 / 4
36
I like listening to music.
My sister goes shopping on Saturday.
Every day, I have to do two hours of homework.
In July, we always go on holiday to France.
Yesterday, I learned a lot in the German lesson.

127. Paper 4: Writing (Foundation)
Sample answers:
1.1 Es gibt acht junge Leute.
1.2 Sie sind im Park.
1.3 Der Park ist schmutzig.
1.4 Sie sammeln Müll.
1.5 Es gibt Flaschen und Papier.
2 Sample answer:
Ich bin sportlich und spiele jeden Tag Basketball.
Ich gehe am Wochenende zu dem Café im Park. Ich mag das Eis.
Es gibt gute Geschäfte in der Stadt, und ich gehe gern einkaufen.
Ich gehe mit meinen Freundinnen ins Kino.
Zu Hause sehe ich fern oder spiele Videospiele mit meinem Bruder.
3.1 hat
3.2 Ich
3.3 neues
3.4 ist
3.5 Der
4 Sample answer:
Dieses Jahr bin ich fünfzehn Jahre alt.
Wir wohnen in einer kleinen Stadt.
Ich denke, dass Mathe ein schweres / schwieriges Fach ist.
Sie will heute nach der Schule einkaufen gehen.
Letzten Samstag sind wir auf ein Konzert gegangen.
5 (a) Sample answer:
Ich versuche, gesund zu essen und esse jeden Tag fünf Stück Obst und Gemüse. Ich esse jeden Morgen Brot mit Käse und Obst zum Frühstück. Ich bin sportlich und gehe oft schwimmen, denn ich finde es entspannend.
Gestern habe ich zu Mittag Hähnchen mit Gemüse und Pommes frites gegessen und Wasser getrunken. Am Nachmittag habe ich nach der Schule im Café Kuchen gegessen, weil meine Freundin Geburtstag hatte.
Heute Abend werde ich ein bisschen fernsehen und dann in meinem Schlafzimmer Musik hören und lesen. Dann werde ich früh ins Bett gehen.
5 (b) Sample answer:
Mein Handy ist sehr wichtig für mich, und ich benutze es jeden Tag. Mit meinem Handy kann ich immer mit meinen Freunden in Kontakt bleiben. Ich finde Simsen so schnell und praktisch. Ich höre auch Musik mit meinem Handy.
Gestern habe ich das Internet für meine Hausaufgaben benutzt. Ich habe auch eine gute Webseite gefunden, auf man Fremdsprachen üben kann.

In der Zukunft werde ich die sozialen Medien benutzen – ich möchte lustige Fotos teilen und ich will wissen, was meine Freunde tun, wenn wir nicht mehr in der Schule zusammen sind.

128. Paper 1: Listening (Higher)

1.1 C	1.2 A	2.1 C	2.2 A
2.3 B	2.4 B	3 A	4 D
5 F	6 B		

7.1 (his / Finn and Lena's) stepmother
7.2 red trousers
8 P+N
9 N
10 P+N
11 P
12 2 / F
13 1 / N
14 stepfather / cross / angry
15 lazy / helps
16 unfair / unjust / kitchen
17 B
18 A+B
19 A
20.1 He portrays (difficult) feelings / emotions. / He is honest.
20.2 It's a fact / neither an advantage nor a disadvantage.
20.3 Her strong (singing) voice / She sings in several languages.
21 E
22 B
23 A
24.1 They are on an island (in a river).
24.2 ancient history / 19th-century art
24.3 Visitors can better understand the museum collections.

Dictation
1 Mein Lieblingsfach ist Geschichte.
2 In der Zukunft möchte ich Journalist werden.
3 Auf der Party haben wir **Limonade** getrunken.
4 Er hat ein gutes **Verhältnis** zu seiner Freundin.
5 Sport ist mir wichtig.

132. Paper 2: Speaking (Higher)

1 Role play
Sample answer:
Teacher: Du sprichst mit deinem österreichischen Freund. Ich bin dein Freund.
Teacher: Wie findest du deine Stadt?
Student: Ich finde meine Stadt ein bisschen langweilig.
Teacher: Interessant.
Student: Wo wohnst du?
Teacher: Ich wohne in einem Dorf.
Teacher: Was gibt es für Touristen in deiner Gegend?
Student: Es gibt eine alte Kirche und ein Restaurant.
Teacher: Schön.
Teacher: Wie sind die Geschäfte in deiner Stadt?
Student: Wir haben nicht viele Geschäfte. Der Supermarkt ist klein.
Teacher: Aha.
Teacher: Was wirst du dieses Wochenende in der Stadt machen?
Student: Ich werde in dem Park laufen und dann einkaufen gehen.
Teacher: Sehr gut.

2 Reading aloud and sample answers to follow-on questions:
(a) Ich habe einige sehr gute Lehrer und Lehrerinnen, aber andere sind streng. Diese Stunden sind nicht so gut.
(b) Ich mag viele Fächer, aber mein bestes Fach ist Erdkunde. Ich finde es interessant, denn ich lerne gern über die Welt.

(c) Hausaufgaben sind wichtig, weil wir viel lernen müssen, aber es ist manchmal schwer, zu Hause zu arbeiten.
(d) Ich weiß nicht genau, aber ich möchte auf die Uni gehen und eine gute Arbeit finden.

3 Photo card
Sample answer:
Auf dem Foto gibt es vier Jugendliche, zwei Mädchen und zwei Jungen. Sie sitzen draußen und sprechen und alle haben ein Handy. Ein Junge hat kurze Haare und trägt eine schwarze Jacke. Ein Mädchen hat lange braune Haare. Sie lachen und sehen glücklich aus. Ich denke, sie benutzen das Internet oder soziale Medien.
Auf dem Foto sehe ich eine Frau und einen Mann. Sie sind keine jungen Leute. Sie haben einen Laptop und machen etwas online. Sie sind glücklich. Die Frau hat blonde Haare und trägt ein weißes T-Shirt und eine braune Hose. Der Mann hat graue Haare und trägt ein blaues Hemd. Sie sind zu Hause im Wohnzimmer.
Sample answers to follow-on questions:
(a) Mein Handy ist sehr wichtig für mich. Ich spreche mit Freunden, ich schicke Nachrichten und E-Mails und ich höre Musik.
(b) Ich mag soziale Medien. Ich sehe, was meine Freundinnen machen, und ich folge meinen Lieblingsstars.
(c) Ich lade Filme herunter, ich sehe Musikvideos an und ich finde Informationen für meine Hausaufgaben.
(d) Ich habe gestern auf Instagram ein Online-Konzert von der Band Meursault gesehen. Das war toll.
(e) Ich finde Online-Einkaufen sehr praktisch, weil es mehr Produkte gibt und weil sie oft billiger sind als in einem Geschäft in der Stadt.
(f) In den Osterferien war ich zu Hause. Ich musste für die Prüfungen lernen, aber ich habe auch meine Freunde gesehen. Wir sind zweimal ins Kino gegangen und haben eine Geburtstagsparty gehabt.
(g) In den Sommerferien werde ich mit meiner Familie nach Spanien fahren. Meine Tante hat ein Haus am Strand, und wir werden eine Woche dort verbringen.
(h) In meiner Stadt gibt es ein Fitness-Studio, viele Cafés und einen Park, wo man Sport treiben kann.
(i) Ich bin mit meinen Freunden auf ein Konzert gegangen. Es war toll.
(j) Ich denke, ich möchte in der Zukunft in einer Großstadt leben, weil das Leben dort Spaß macht. Ich würde gern in London arbeiten, aber ich muss zuerst einen Job finden.

133. Paper 3: Reading (Higher)

1 B / C	2 3 / 4	3 D	4 E
5 B	6 A		

7 She was 17.
8 Best young actress
9 An action thriller

10 A	11 P+N	12 P	13 N

14 To improve her language skills

15 A	16 B	17 B	18 B
19 A	20 A+B	21 B	22 A+B
23 B	24 B	25 A	26 B
27 A	28 A+B		

29 pointless / senseless
30 polluted
31 rubbish / litter
32 water / energy
33 careful / attentive / mindful / aware

34 C	35 M+L	36 M	37 L

38 M+L
39 At home we eat together in the evening and talk about the day. I like sport and I play with my team three times a week. When / If / Whenever it's possible, I like to spend time with my friends.

157

Next year, I hope to study science(s) at university.
Recently, I found a great present for my stepmother on the internet / online.

139. Paper 4: Writing (Higher)

1. Ich esse immer gesundes Essen.
   Er interessiert sich nicht für Stars.
   Ich hoffe, diesen Sommer eine große Geburtstagsparty zu haben.
   Wir verstehen alle, dass es gefährlich ist, zu viel Zeit online zu verbringen.
   Ich habe ein paar neue Freunde kennengelernt, als ich im Urlaub war.

2. (a) Sample answer:
   Ich versuche, gesund zu essen und esse jeden Tag fünf Stück Obst und Gemüse. Ich esse jeden Morgen Brot mit Käse und Obst zum Frühstück. Ich bin sportlich und gehe oft schwimmen, denn ich finde es entspannend.
   Gestern habe ich zu Mittag Hähnchen mit Gemüse und Pommes frites gegessen und Wasser getrunken. Am Nachmittag habe ich nach der Schule im Café Kuchen gegessen, weil meine Freundin Geburtstag hatte.
   Heute Abend werde ich ein bisschen fernsehen und dann in meinem Schlafzimmer Musik hören und lesen. Dann werde ich früh ins Bett gehen.

   (b) Sample answer:
   Mein Handy ist sehr wichtig für mich, und ich benutze es jeden Tag. Mit meinem Handy kann ich immer mit meinen Freunden in Kontakt bleiben. Ich finde Simsen so schnell und praktisch. Ich höre auch Musik mit meinem Handy.
   Gestern habe ich das Internet für meine Hausaufgaben benutzt. Ich habe auch eine gute Webseite gefunden, auf der man Fremdsprachen üben kann.
   In der Zukunft werde ich die sozialen Medien benutzen – ich möchte lustige Fotos teilen und ich will wissen, was meine Freunde tun, wenn wir nicht mehr in der Schule zusammen sind.

3. (a) Sample answer:
   Heute haben viele junge Leute ein glückliches Leben, aber auf der anderen Seite gibt es auch manchmal viel Druck. In der Schule müssen sie hart arbeiten und viel lernen, um in den Prüfungen erfolgreich zu sein. Aus diesem Grund denke ich, dass genug Freizeit total notwendig ist, damit Jugendliche nicht immer unter Druck stehen und ihr Leben genießen können, ohne krank zu werden. Für mich ist Freizeit wichtig, da ich eine Pause machen kann. Ich verbringe gern diese Zeit mit Familie und Freunden und vergesse kurz die ganze Schularbeit. Ich finde es nützlich, sich zu bewegen, weil das auch gut für die Gesundheit ist.
   In der Zukunft werde ich bestimmt eine Arbeitsstelle haben und vielleicht auch eine Familie und Kinder. Es wird dann wahrscheinlich schwieriger sein, freie Momente zu finden. Ich werde trotzdem versuchen, nicht die ganze Zeit zu arbeiten, damit ich fit bleibe und manchmal mit Freunden ausgehen und Spaß haben kann.

   (b) Sample answer:
   Ich mache mir Sorgen um die Umwelt und um die Zukunft unserer Welt. Man liest täglich über die schlimme Situation, die jetzt weltweit existiert, wo Klimaveränderung mit immer höheren Temperaturen ein ernstes Problem ist. Viele Leute denken, es ist schon zu spät, etwas Positives zu tun, und machen deshalb nichts, um die Situation zu verbessern. Ich bin gegen dieses Denken. Meiner Meinung nach können wir und müssen wir alle die Verantwortung teilen, die Umwelt für die nächste Generation zu schützen.
   Ich habe immer versucht, umweltfreundlich zu sein. Ich fahre kein Auto und bin in den letzten Jahren nie mit meiner Familie mit dem Flugzeug geflogen, um Luftverschmutzung zu reduzieren. Letzte Woche bin ich entweder mit dem Fahrrad zur Schule gefahren oder zu Fuß gegangen. Mit meiner Klasse habe ich in der Stadt Müll gesammelt, um unsere Umgebung sauberer und angenehmer zu machen. Es hat Spaß gemacht, diese freiwillige Arbeit mit Freunden zu machen.